FLYING CHICKADEE

THRIVE!

Shahana Dattagupta wishes to be the catalyst for the highest (creative) potential of others, to create a thriving world, one being at a time. She uses various mediums to this end: writing, visual art, music, theater, and architectural design. Shahana considers Seattle the place of her rebirth, and after a decade in her picturesque womb, 'home' has come to be associated with both India's vigorous monsoons and Seattle's incessant rain, both the lights of Diwali and the warmth of Thanksgiving, and both the Tricolor on August 15th and The Star Spangled Banner on July 4th. She still tears up inexplicably about the Partition of India and Pakistan in 1947. And she really does believe that love is *always* the answer.

Shahana has previously written *Ten Avatars*, a debut fiction collection exploring 'avatars' of womanhood through her transcultural lens. She is also co-founding-editor of the monthly 'zine *Courageous Creativity*, in which stories of courage, creativity and change from diverse contributors all over the world are curated.

THRIVE!

Falling in Love with Life

Shahana Dattagupta

Flying Chickadee

ISBN-13:
978-0615533704 (*Thrive!*)

ISBN-10:
0615533701

First printing, November 2011
Flying Chickadee
PO Box 30021, Seattle, WA 98113-0021
www.flyingchickadee.com

Some essays in this book were first published (in different form) in the author's online blog *Reflections and Revelations* (www.reflectionsandrevelations.com).

Chapter images and author photographs ©2011 by Siddhartha Saha
Concept for chapter images by Shahana Dattagupta
Cover image ©2011 by Shahana Dattagupta (in collaboration with Jason Week)
Reader reviews by Harold Soans and Archana Verma
Editing and proofing by Shirin Subhani

For my parents, Ranu and Sushanta, for gifting my birth

and

For Andrew, for gifting my rebirth

PROLOGUE

"There are two ways to live your life. One is as though nothing is a miracle. The other is as though everything is a miracle."

– Albert Einstein

On December 28, 2005, I had stood facing death. I had been suicidal for a period of a few weeks, and on that day I thought that it would be so much easier to die than to struggle with my suffering a single moment longer. The year before, at the age of thirty, I had emerged from a long history of emotional and physical violence beginning in my childhood and extending into an eight-year marriage. The divorce had become final in August, and all the symptoms of post-traumatic stress disorder had only begun to emerge in the recent months.

It had all started in early 2004, leading up to my thirtieth birthday, when a strange, unexplained power had begun to stir me. I had felt a peculiar disembodiment from everything I knew to be familiar, as if the life I was living – married, owning a home, working in a large corporate office – was entirely somebody else's. That my marriage had become grossly violent, that my body had become seriously ill from all the hiding and pretense and repression, somehow hadn't really figured in this experience…it seemed to be about something other than all that, something mysteriously powerful, calling and pulling me towards it.

And then, as if to provide the final shove, I had found my soul ruthlessly and startlingly bared in the mirror, in my friend Andrew. I had thought of him as my 'best friend' for a couple of years, but until just then, I had been comfortably oblivious to the connection, significance and transformative power of his presence in my life. Unwittingly, by just being who he is, he had said uncanny, telepathic things to stir me from my coma, to wake me from my stupor, to spark my enthusiasm, to rekindle my fire for creativity, to relentlessly reflect to me, my purer, essential nature as a vibrant, creative being. I had been terrified, at being irreversibly exposed, and there had been no turning back.

In the ensuing turmoil of the separation and divorce, it had been easy to desperately cling to this transformative connection with my 'twin soul,' and insist that it should convert into a relationship that would somehow redeem my past. But at the time, this was not to be, and the hiatus we agreed upon felt like an unbearable rupture, a staggering loss on top of the heap of rubble I was already grappling with. It was as if I had barely glimpsed my soul, and it was already being emptied out. I found myself staring into an enormous, gaping, black void, expressive of the total sum of grief and loss I had experienced much of my life, but with whose weight and significance I had never allowed myself to fully connect.

On top of all this, my 'coming out' as a recipient of abuse had encouraged several others – family, friends, acquaintances, and even strangers – to share their own abuse-ridden pasts with me. In particular, my younger sister revealed to me her horrific teenage experience with continuous cruelty and rape, resulting in two dangerously terminated pregnancies. It felt impossible to reconcile with all the violence and destruction that had occurred in such close quarters, festering for so long as well-guarded secrets. Now I carried around the grief and shock from others' suffering amalgamated with my own, a collective testament of human frailty.

Then, a favorite uncle – my father's younger brother – had died unexpectedly at the young age of fifty-eight. The shock of his untimely passing had acted as the proverbial straw that broke the camel's back. Flailing in a web of repetitive nightmares with twisted acts of violence, chronic sleeplessness and depression, I experienced an excruciating hopelessness that cracked open my chest and nearly stopped my breathing. I remember vividly those moments when death danced in front of me like a compelling, alluring, enticing force, drawing me towards it with the promise of an ultimate, eternal relief.

And then something miraculous happened that day. In a desperate bid for fresh air to combat the suicidal designs racing through my mind, I began walking around and around the block of my downtown condominium building. Outside, the trees looked greener than believable in Seattle's relentlessly rainy winter. The typically gray, December light had a special, uncharacteristic luminescence. Then, I began to see words and phrases everywhere: on passing vans with advertisements, on the posters in the retail windows, in the print in the newspaper stand...all leaping out at me in synchronized significance. Woven together, the words carried a unified message: They were, quite literally, beckoning me to *choose life*! Then I had a luminescent vision of a giant palm, with fingers reaching out to my small hand like a big, big, parent might reach to Her little one, Her creation, lovingly beckoning me to stand up, reassuring me that I could, indeed, walk again. I received the message that I am here to *create* my life, with unfettered and unlimited love.

I returned home and began to cry. I had cried many, many tears of sorrow, pain and anger in the last year-and-a-half, but they had been nothing like this powerful but peaceful, full-bodied flow. My sobs were not from grief this time; they were from realization, from understanding…from a powerful awakening. In an instant my entire life passed before my eyes, and in every scene, I saw the big hand formed in blessing over my head; I had just never noticed it there before. It was like watching a surreal movie flashback. There it was – the blessing – in every frame, as if I had been hoodwinked into missing it in previous screenings, and it was now being revealed to me frame by frame, for the very first time. "You have always been with me!" I exclaimed out loud, in disbelief. "Indeed, I have!" echoed a response from within my being.

In that instant I knew that the initial awakening to my purer nature in the mirror soul of Andrew was only the first step in a deeper, fuller awakening to my Higher Power. I saw that the very purpose of such a reflection, which had dismantled and shattered all the masks I had layered on through the years, was to catalyze a rebirth, so I may connect with my highest potential *within my own wholeness*. So, of course, running immediately from one relationship to another was not the answer! I became flooded with immense awe, gratitude, compassion, peace, and love.

On December 28, 2005, I was reborn. It was the day of my rebirth because I made a conscious choice to live, dying to the constructs of a self that had been, thus far, based on false narratives. It was the day of my rebirth also because I chose to submit to the unknown, undefined, and unproved: a mysterious, miraculous higher intelligence. In one inexplicable lightning strike, I understood that I *must* live, that my Higher Power is right here with me, and that I am made in the likeness of my Creator and given Her creative powers! *I am powerfully able at every moment to co-create my life.* Until that moment I had been surviving life, experiencing it happening *to* me. In that moment of awakening, I understood that life is created *through* me. I took full responsibility, and embarked on a practice of thriving, my heart still fully cracked open…with love.

Shahana Dattagupta
June 26, 2009

Contents

INTRODUCTION

INTRODUCTION

"In your light I learn how to love.
In your beauty, how to make poems.
You dance inside my chest, where no one sees you,
But sometimes I do, and that sight becomes this art."

– Rumi

T*hrive!* is about creating life in its every facet – personal, professional, relational, emotional, intellectual, physical or spiritual – using pure love as the only creative force. *Thrive!* is therefore, my unfolding love story with life, continuing beyond the bounds of this book; between these pages, I attempt only to give you a snapshot in time.

This love story became conscious of itself when I saw my purer nature reflected in the mirror: in my twin-soul,[1] Andrew, and this deeply moving experience catalyzed an unexpected and rapid disintegration of my life of illusion and pretense. By shedding layers of my false self through this singular, transformative, telepathic connection that I can only understand as divine intervention, a tremendous awakening occurred. Then, in spite of (–and I'm convinced, because of–) 'loss' experienced in the material plane of this relationship, the story blossomed into a love-story with my Higher Power, with my awakened self, with my creativity, with other beings, with entire communities, with collective human potential…and through it all, with life itself.

This story, therefore, is offered to every soul, because every soul has love at its core, and is the powerful, evergreen creator of its own life, whether its physical and intellectual owner is conscious of this amazing gift, or not. Every soul has an innate seed for a thriving, creative life, no matter what its past or present external context might be. You may consider yours a fairly 'typical' life, with mostly happy and ordinary circumstances. Or, you may believe you've experienced extraordinary circumstances, uplifting or depressing, or both.

---

1. Because I use the term 'twin soul' in several places, it merits the only paragraph-length footnote of this book. In 2004, I made up the term instinctively as the only appropriate descriptor of the person in whom I experienced a mysterious, miraculous and telepathic reflection of my higher, truer nature. Nothing else seemed to fit. Far down the road, I was rather stunned to discover that the term 'twin soul' (or 'twin flame') is used by many to describe similar experiences of transformative spiritual resonance and unity with another being, frequently but not necessarily, of opposite gender. It is said that whether these relationships manifest as couplehood or not, they are characterized by pure, essential, unconditional love, and are meant to serve a higher purpose for the benefit of humanity and the Universe. The most documented psychic of the 20th Century, Edgar Cayce, also called the 'sleeping prophet' and 'the father of holistic medicine,' has written about twin souls. Now there are a growing number of religious, spiritual and mystical references to the phenomenon of twin souls, many of which uncannily correlate with my direct experience, sometimes word-for-word.

You may have suffered violence or abuse in your childhood, in romantic relationships or at work; you may yourself have abused alcohol, drugs or other beings; you may have suffered losses of material or loved ones; you may have experienced a serious injury or a grave illness; your community or identity may have been exploited, rejected or discriminated against in this world.

No matter what your particular story is, we are all survivors of *something*: of our births, of our childhoods and their conditionings, of our early-adulthoods and their struggles, of our single or family or working lives, of disease, of bereavement, of injustice, of circumstances. In surviving what we perceive as life's circumstances, we pick up baggage along the way. Over time we make this baggage a part of our identity, and we become afraid to dismantle what we believe is integral to us. We are afraid because, paradoxically, this baggage has become our strong suit, our toolkit for survival. Because it has helped us survive, we carry it around like a dear, inseparable companion, convinced that it will help us again in the future. We don't notice that this toolkit has become so heavy that it is no less than shackles, holding us back, dragging us down!

If and when our inner light turns on, we see otherwise. We choose to take responsibility and begin to *create* our own life: *to thrive*. We realize that the accumulated baggage and survival toolkit are the very millstones hanging around our necks, impeding our evolution, clouding our vision, and interfering with our amazing and innate ability to create new reality, moment-to-moment. *We discover that surviving [2] is actually antithetic to thriving!* To make a quantum leap into thriving, we must set aside our weighty survival toolkit, *die* to the past and self-constructs, and submit fully, implicitly and terrifyingly to the mysterious, miraculous unknown.

Presented as my "falling in love with life," *Thrive!* is a collection of personal stories and essays with reflections, revelations, insights, and epiphanies from experiences in the last seven years, following the singular moment in which I consciously chose life and began practicing the art of thriving. The stories and essays are organized in seven chapters loosely outlining stages in my practice: *Centering, Consciousness, Compassion, Choice, Creativity, Connectedness,* and *Commitment.* This sequential arrangement does not strictly correlate

---

2. Throughout this book, I use the term 'surviving' to connote the surviving *mindset*, rather than the actual act of surviving a particular event or set of events in one's life. The act of surviving is an isolated response to a life- or soul-threatening situation, whereas the surviving mindset is a way of thinking about one's life, an *idea* of life as a struggle against adversity, scarcity, injustice or peril, and the constructing of narratives based on such a past or present.

with the chronology of the specific life experiences. Also, while the chapters are presented as stages, the Seven Cs also occur concurrently or in iterative cycles in my life, sometimes within the period of a single day, or just a couple of hours! I present them in a linear, ordered sequence largely due to narrative necessity. The chapters and essays can be read in any order, though they are bound to have a unique resonance when read in the one presented.

Consistent with the central message in *Thrive!*, is the overarching insight that *the past that brought me (to) this present is essentially quite irrelevant.* Yes, there are references to violence and suffering, to grief and devastation, to love and loss … but as I often like to say: *One must break down to break through.* The circumstances in my life were the compost – to borrow Dr. Bernie Siegel's term from his loving book *Prescriptions for Living* – which afforded the rich fodder for my awakening to my Higher Power, and to my creativity, purpose, and highest potential. Therefore, the sole role of the narrative of the past is to act as context for my insights, and as a means for storytelling. While the references to my past, including to the last seven years, provide a means for readers to identify and relate with, they do not form my identity.

This book is intended for all those ready to access their highest potential, ready to take responsibility for creating their own lives moment-to-moment, and ready to thrive with love, purpose, creativity, peace, health and joy. The insights offered here are drawn from both personal and professional contexts; so, I imagine that they might help you in either context as well. But this book is an urgent, heartfelt call to recognize yourselves as whole, integrated, creative beings, instead of compartmentalized aspects in separate roles and realms. I hope that the sharing of my little stories and related insights will move you to turn whatever compost you have in your life into rich fodder, and to harness every drop of creative potential with which you were surely born.

Oh, and one more thing! There is nothing in this book that the great masters of all traditions have not already taught through the centuries, or more importantly, that life itself might not teach you if you simply become still and listen. These stories and related insights are simply my account of timeless lessons, narrated through (the limitations of) my particular temporal, cultural, intellectual, emotional, spiritual and experiential lens. They are intended to lovingly kindle and catalyze your own insights, through your own direct experience, and not as advice or guidance. I gift these stories, with much love, to all those who wish to receive.

Here's to your higher calling: *to thrive!*

For Robb and Rachael

1.
CENTERING

Centering is the act of remembering and reclaiming my innate ability to look after, nurture and heal myself, a divine gift which is always, already available.

I believe my instincts, I trust my Higher Power

Trusting the Universe:
Angels Everywhere!

"There is guidance for each of us, and by lowly listening, we shall hear the right word. Certainly there is a right for you that needs no choice on your part. Place yourself in the middle of the stream of power and wisdom which flows into your life. Then, without effort, you are impelled to truth and to perfect contentment."

– Ralph Waldo Emerson

In the eighth year of my marriage, leading up to my turning thirty in May of 2004, an entirely unexpected and inexplicable calling began to consume me, one that I couldn't name, but one that called to me with an acute urgency to venture deep within. My husband had left for India on a month-long, work-related sabbatical, and the space and silence allowed the powerful, overwhelming force to take over me at lightning speed, leaving the 'usual me' totally out of control.

I found myself giving in to an instinctive whimsy, painting with acrylics sitting sprawled on the wood floor, just like I used to as a child growing up in India in cramped apartments. Deep crimsons and oranges, bright yellows and greens, and stark blacks burst through my brushes, splashing the canvas, creating beauty and form with vehemence and conviction.[3] I found myself beginning to sing again after years, small tunes creating tiny, yet timeless moments of empty space in my typically clogged and racing mind. I went out and about, alone or with others, doing little things I don't remember anymore. All I know is that something else, some other unnamed and unrecognizable power, was suddenly captain of my ship.

When my husband returned from his trip, he declared that I had become someone else, unrecognizable to him. This 'about-turn' that he perceived was, to him, a grave betrayal, and he rapidly became volatile, swinging wildly between tearful tantrums and outbursts

---

3. Six years later, this painting, titled *Cracking India*, became the cover of my first book, *Ten Avatars*! The title of the painting referenced the rising religious divisiveness in India at the time, with the Bharatiya Janata Party in power in the Central Government, but at the personal level, it represented my own cracking up and disintegration.

of violent rage. The familiar patterns he had suppressed for the last year or so, quickly resurfaced. But this time around I refused to engage. I don't know what it was, but I had absolutely nothing more left to say, nothing more to plead, convince, or argue. My old self had simply given up control, and the inexplicable force, which much down the road I began calling my Higher Power, had taken over.

Thereafter things disintegrated with an unbelievable rapidity, all at once in slow-motion and in fast-forward. My husband unwittingly illuminated my path by his violent words and allegations, accusing me of having affairs, and of plotting to live separately and get a divorce, long before I had really had the chance to consider these options myself! And before I knew what had hit me, on the day after Thanksgiving, I left my home of four years and marriage of eight.

I lived for over a month with newly-made friends, a married couple with two young boys. 'Newly-made' is an understatement: I had met Robb for the first time barely two weeks prior to making this huge, life-changing choice, and I met his lovely wife, Rachael, the evening I moved in to their home! Robb was Andrew's childhood friend, and perhaps in the vein of my twin-soul connection with Andrew, Robb and I too had instantly felt an old, familiar friendship from the moment we'd met. Only two weeks later, over a follow-up lunch with Robb intended to discuss his interest in tabla lessons, I had suddenly found myself sharing my current state of life with him. And without blinking an eye, he had insisted that I move in with his family!

Amazingly, this type of inexplicable generosity wasn't limited to Robb; it appeared to be the general trend during this period of my life. Since the day a few months ago that I had known in my heart that I was being called in a new direction, not only had Andrew become a powerful mirror for my soul, but mere acquaintances and complete strangers had also begun to emerge from the woodwork to help me, to be my signposts, to act as my angels.

During the time I lived with my newfound family, at the office too, I was temporarily assigned to work in a different design studio: a new 'home-base at work,' if you will. Given that this was a large, global design firm, with the Seattle office alone being three-hundred-strong, I was just as uprooted in my work setting as I was in my home setting, feeling like I was camping out in both places. At first the upheaval, uncertainty and itinerant existence were intensely unsettling. After years of knowing, planning and charting everything, and always being 'in-control' – you'd be surprised how controlling one has to be, to keep up facades and live with tormenting secrets – I had no idea how to navigate this time of not-knowing, not-planning, and not being in-control.

As I relinquished more control though, several people in the new studio came forward to assist me in unexpected ways. A senior project manager, Charles, not known for the best social skills – he had a military background and was used to growling out orders – became my quiet, caring protector after he caught me incessantly on the phone or email with my raging, spurned spouse one day, and I became forced to confide in him. "You are like my sister, and I am here to protect you," Charles declared solemnly through his awkward blinking, words that one might expect in a traditional Indian setting, not in an American, corporate workplace.

Two other colleagues, both previously nurse practitioners who now did design consulting for large hospital projects, made themselves available to me. Lynn became an informal counselor of sorts, Tammy offered me her home if I wanted an alternative place to stay, and both gave me daily hugs. The office manager Lisa left me cards, flowers and candy, and never failed to make me smile with her beautiful smile and sparkling blue eyes, and constant words of encouragement. Another senior manager, Nancy, reminded me that one of the reasons we work in teams is so that we can cover for and support one another. I should never stay after dark to finish pending work but instead, stay safe, warm and get plenty of rest, she suggested gently but firmly. My colleague Bonnie found me an amazingly resonant psychotherapist, Anya. And another colleague, Megan, introduced me to a massage and Reiki practitioner of magical talent, David.[4] In the able and loving hands of my two therapists, Anya and David, I gradually began to find my footing.

I had similar experiences when out and about. On the days I set out apartment hunting, scanning openings in Belltown, Pioneer Square and the International District, the apartment managers were, quite inexplicably, more than just polite. They extended themselves beyond call of duty to show me the best possibilities, and to bend their rules, offering me extended timelines and lowered deposits. From the apartment manager to the hairdresser, from the bank manager to the bus driver, everyone showered me with their kindest gazes and warmest smiles.

---

4. David specializes in cancer rehabilitation, and has the incredible gift of using his hands like scanners, to feel vibrational frequency variations in the body and thereby detect unusual occurrences. He was once the massage therapist for the renowned band *Pearl Jam*, traveling with them on world tours!

The more my life of secrets dismantled and disintegrated, the fewer pretenses I kept up. The more I allowed my vulnerabilities to show, the more people stepped out of their ordinary scripts to become my angels.[5] I couldn't fully understand it, but I did become aware that what I considered my weakness, others experienced as courage, and both these others and I were transformed in those moments of vulnerability by a divine grace, which channeled itself through our incredible, healing interactions.

With all that was intensely familiar already relinquished, it might seem that I would feel the need to grasp at something or someone from my old life, but instead, I began to experience a strange comfort at this drastic, clean severance. This was the seed of my growing awareness, that from the moment I had let go of control and taken the leap, the Universe had stepped forward to catch me in its arms. I began to realize what 'a leap of faith' really meant, and quickly recognized people who may have appeared as strangers, as my angels. And as my faith in the Universe deepened, I became aware that any time we are desperately stuck in an apparently choice-less situation, it is a sign that we have put very little faith in the Universe, and far too much emphasis on personal, fear-based control. It was a startling insight that would go on to shape much of my future course.

Accepting the Tears:
Pain Versus Suffering

"Tears are the summer showers to the soul."

– Alfred Austin

I often sat in my friends' bright kitchen, sipping a cup of ginger tea and staring into their grassy yard with the big, beautiful Dogwood tree, charmed by their two-year-old

---

5. Much later I pondered how my husband also showed me the way with his behavior – out the door – and this, quite ironically, makes him one of my angels too!

gurgling at me from his high-chair and their older boy, about five, studying me with quiet concern. It felt like a preordained homecoming, with a sense of utter safety and familiarity that I had never experienced even around my own parents growing up. I don't know if it was because of this profound feeling of safety, or the immensely overwhelming nature of the step I had just taken, that a peculiar rhythm laced my days. Time passed differently than I was used to – every moment seemed long and eternal, deliberate and full – quite different from the fast-paced blur I was accustomed to in my now dismantled married-and-working life. And I was never sure what I really felt; sometimes I giggled uncontrollably with the little boys, at other times I cried deluges of tears. I either talked a whole lot, or I fell into spells of deep silence.

The days I made it in to work had their very own quality, too. The tears often hit ten to fifteen minutes apart, and when I was lucky, I had up to two hours at a stretch to get some work done, before they came bursting through again. Routinely, I had to excuse myself from large team or client meetings and run to the restroom, cry out the tears that had welled up, and then run back to rejoin the session.

I felt deathly afraid, not so much of what I had undertaken, but of the tears themselves: Ironically, to actually feel the devastation was scarier than the devastation itself. To face the tears – to make space for them, to allow them to flow – seemed harder than the reasons and stories behind them. In fact, the reasons behind the tears were quite obscured and abstract.

Yes, I had jumped ship from everything that was familiar, had broken an entrenched pattern of violence, and had parted from a long, complex relationship that had also had love, but on each occasion that the tears burst through, there were no immediate, tangible reasons for them in that particular instant. They just came, like unannounced, uninvited, unwelcome guests, with whom I simply had to put up. My rational brain, which I was to learn later, had been unhealthily dominating my instincts and body for most of my thirty years, struggled hard, flailing its arms and throwing tantrums at these unwelcome guests. Why were they here? Why didn't they go away? What had happened to the 'strong' and 'in-charge' me, who could pick up and move on with life no matter what? Eventually, I (and my rational brain) gave in. These guests, it appeared, were here to stay. And there was no telling when they were going to leave; it seemed they were here on a mission, and were going to stay as long as they needed to fulfill it.[6]

---

6. It took two full years for my tears to taper out and stop flowing!

By this time, I was working on a significant project for The Boeing Company, on what went on to be my most important work, from nearly a decade in the architectural design field. We were creating a design concept based on organizational research of the company and the factory, and the core team I was working with was largely male. All three men on the team – Scott, Jason and Tim – seemed to have no trouble with my tears. In fact, like all the other angels suddenly in my surrounds during this time, they implicitly let me know that it was all right to be, however I was being. The design-lead, Scott, with whom I went on to cultivate a lasting and important friendship, even encouraged me to consider our project room a safe space to express my grief as and when I needed!

So I let go, allowing the tears to come and go as they pleased, excusing myself whenever I could, or simply letting them flow in others' witness when running away was not necessary or possible. Eventually, my tears became like any other necessary bodily function, which need not be explained, which simply needs to be attended to, in order to move on to the next thing at hand.

This process forced me, for the first time ever, to step out of my rational brain and its incessant need to analyze and explain everything, and simply *be*. And, I began to slowly become aware that my 'unreasonable' tears were the means for my body and psyche to express its pain, not just the pain I was feeling right then, but years of suppressed and repressed pain. It was a natural process of cleansing.

I began to welcome these guests now, making special room for them, even being grateful for them, and learning to simply observe them. With this approach, magically, they didn't stay very long at a time! They came just as suddenly as before, but they seemed to do their bit and depart, like quick tropical showers that leave everything fresh, green, and sweet-smelling. In the times between the tears, I became more focused and efficient than ever before. I felt light.[7]

Then one day I realized: Whenever I struggled against the tears, fearing, resisting, denying, or being embarrassed by them, what I experienced was suffering. But when I let

---

7. I must mention here that around this time, from obsessive Internet searches for answers about the psychology of abuse, I ran into an incredible gift of an e-book titled *Tears and Healing*. In it, an engineer, Richard Skerritt, traces his journey of healing via tears, after emerging from a marriage in which his disordered wife had him convinced through years of mental abuse that he was sexually abusing his own children! That a scientific-minded, 'rational' male had stumbled upon the truth and power of his tears was a wonderful, encouraging, and affirming parallel to my own journey and realizations.

them flow, what I experienced was simply pain. Pain, like joy, I began to see, is purely an emotion, meant to be fully felt and experienced. There is no inherent good or bad to it. As soon as I feared the pain and ascribed it a negative value – "it is bad" – it became suffering. Suffering is a mental, psychological and social phenomenon, while pain is a physical, emotional and spiritual one. Pain, by itself, has no meaning. Suffering, on the other hand, is loaded with meaning, meaning that makes it linger, perpetuate and then take a dangerous, addictive stronghold.

The more I allowed myself to acknowledge and feel pain, the less I suffered. I had stumbled upon a simple but paradoxical truth: Feeling and accepting pain is the first step to freedom from suffering!

Listening to the Body:
Matter over Mind

"The more consciousness you bring into the body, the stronger the immune system becomes. It is as if every cell awakens and rejoices. The body loves your attention. It is also a potent form of self-healing."

– Eckhart Tolle, *The Power of Now*

My experiences with tears provided an opening to a whole new world: to my body. My body revealed itself as that revered home for my spirit and my intellect, whose value and deep wisdom I had thus far barely noticed, let alone remotely harnessed. I had heard phrases such as "living in your head," and friends and colleagues had repeatedly observed, with admiration and awe, how intellectual I was. But neither had the former rung any bells, nor had the latter seemed anything other than a compliment. I had been proud of my superlative intellectual abilities, reserving the term 'intelligence' largely to connote mental acumen, aligned with my upbringing in academically aspiring Indian middle-class society.

My body, on the other hand, I had considered a liability, something I had to will-fully work around. I had suffered from Irritable Bowel Syndrome (IBS) since I had been ten years old (coinciding with a period of sexual abuse I endured for over six months from a family-friend), and I had developed debilitating migraines later in my teens (coinciding with the peak of violent turmoil in my parents' marriage), and subsequently, weight gain, hair loss, and menstrual problems (coinciding with the violence in my own marriage). I also had ongoing knee trouble from cartilage damage in an episode of violence, and later, lower abdominal clenching and spasms after an attack involving my abdomen. Eventually, my colon was diagnosed as 'spastic,' which is a condition often associated with continuous internalization of emotional trauma. Phew! All this before my thirtieth birthday!

So, I had been given signs of a pained, ravaged body all along; but, instead of 'listening' to it and recognizing these so-called illnesses as its messages — no, urgent pleas — I had instead, used my dominating intellect to quell its plaintive cries. "I am fine!" I had told myself and simply carried on, living a life of deceit and dissonance between mind and body. But as I became comfortable with uncertainty, letting go of mental control and making space for my tears, I began to have a heightened awareness about my body, including its subtler senses.

I noticed my breath: how it was, on most occasions, shallow and gasping.[8] I noticed when my heart beat faster, when I broke into a stressful sweat, when my jaw clenched, when my temple pulsed, or when my extremities turned cold. I noticed which sensations converted into a migraine down the road, and which interfered with my sleep. I had felt these types of sensations all along in my life, but now I was tuning into them, with growing awareness of the clues they offered in various contexts, and beginning to — instinctively, not analytically — connect the dots and understand their messages. For instance, I noticed how the tightly-clenched fist in my lower left abdomen, or the sinking stone in my chest flared up when I made certain choices over others.

On the massage table, with David's healing hands working better than sophisti-cated electromagnetic scanners to find areas of knots, distress and damage, I found myself, curiously, releasing more unexplained tears when he worked on my knees or my abdomen. David wasn't in the least bit surprised or concerned. Handing me a tissue, he reassured me

---

8. How *does* one go through life without so much as noticing the very life-force, one's breath? It's a mind-boggling human condition, or shall I say, mind-conditioned human existence! In the ancient Yogic practice of *Pranayama*, currently in tremendous revival in India, it is said that because breath is the very life-force, it is *designed* to cleanse and heal the body: all bodily ailments can be naturally healed simply by the regular and rigorous practice of channeling breath purposefully.

gently, "That is your body-memory, unlocking its blocks and releasing its traumas."

Body-memory? The idea that my body cells had their own memories, separate from what I knew to be memory in my brain, was entirely fascinating, and quite hard to fathom. But then, when more unexplained tears were also unleashed while doing Yoga for the first time since my move to the United States, my talented Caucasian instructor, Blair, calmly assured me that certain Yoga asanas have the capability to unlock trapped emotional energies in the body.

The concept began to sink in, and like the tears I had learned to welcome, I began to acknowledge, and be all right with my body sensations. If my gut clenched in a particular situation, perhaps I simply shouldn't be in it? Might that be what is literally meant by a 'gut-feeling': an instinctive guide to the right path? Previously I would have rationalized away these impulses, but now, whether I knew *why* or not, I began to put all mental reasoning aside to at least listen to the bodily sensations, if not use them as a guide for action, rather than discarding them as mere noise from an inferior, damaged body.

The simple act of listening was transformative: mentally, physically and spiritually. Like my tears, these sensations, when listened to rather than rejected, were able to arrive and depart, doing the needful in their temporary visits. I discovered that when attended to with patience, acknowledgment and love, these sensations are able to play their intended role, acting as gentle signposts from an ancient, bodily wisdom. It is only when they are ignored or repressed that they turn into grosser aggregates – into tumors and into disease – hoping against hope that screaming louder and louder might finally get serious attention!

Along with crying when I wanted to cry, I began doing previously unthinkable things like eating when I was hungry, sleeping when I was sleepy, walking when I felt antsy, taking a break from work and reading at the adjacent Elliot Bay Bookstore when I was tired, and so on. Slowly but surely, a new and wider range of physical sensations began to make itself available to me – like a new vocabulary of words or a new line of fragrances or a fresh palette of colors – that I could now hear, smell, see and appreciate.

Little had I known that over the course of years, I too had unwittingly used and abused my body (just as others had!) as if it were a hollow shell, a mere transport for my spectacular brain, and thereby denied it its rightful, sacred place. But now, I began to see my body as the temple for my soul, the originator of an older, more sophisticated intelligence, and a surefire compass for my life. How often does our lopsided, hyper-rationalized culture advocate 'mind over matter'? Now I realized that a sophisticated, innate wisdom is activated when I place 'matter over mind.' [9]

Finding Balance with Baby Steps:
Center of Gravity

"Take the first step in faith. You don't have to see the whole staircase, just take the first step."

– Martin Luther King Jr.

After about a month of living with my friends Robb and Rachael and their two boys, I found a studio apartment for rent in a modern building in Belltown, just south of the main Seattle downtown corridor, with exposed concrete walls and high ceilings in a five-hundred-square-foot space. The starkness of the concrete, (which had always appealed to my aesthetic sense as an architect), and the barrenness of the space were comforting; they mirrored the empty canvas with which I was starting out once again, and on which, I was hopeful, new things could be painted.

I was close enough to the waterfront to walk along it daily, and witness the Olympic Sculpture Park in construction, its wonderful gliding, earth-hugging, train-track-transcending forms gradually coming into being. On my languid, aimless evening strolls at the edge of the Puget Sound, I sometimes found my body so heavy with grief, that it was difficult to walk, as if I were learning to do so all over again. Although I had learned to acknowledge my body and listen to its cues, it was still tempting to look for an outstretched hand, for reassurances, for guarantees, outside of my own self. I looked to the glorious Mt. Rainier on one side and the setting sun in pink, flaming skies on the other, asking them to be my parents, my guides, my angels.

---

9. I didn't know then that my opening up to body-awareness would eventually lead me to Vipassana, The Buddha's approach to meditation via dedicated and detached observation of body sensations. More on that down the road!

At night I couldn't fall asleep easily, and then experienced what the doctors called 'early-morning awakening': routinely waking up at half-past-two or three in the morning, with the inability to fall back to sleep until about five-thirty, when it was almost time to wake up and get ready for work. Apparently, this is one of the certain symptoms of clinical depression, and they insisted on treating me for it with anti-depressants.

Several months into living alone, one night I had struggled and just managed to fall asleep, when the fire alarm in my high concrete ceiling began to emanate periodic, shrill shrieks. I awoke discombobulated and frightened, unsure of what was happening, the sharp sound cutting through my skin. Then it dawned on me: The battery was running out. I had no way of reaching the alarm so high up there; standing on one of my dining chairs wasn't going to cut it.

In that moment, it was as if the gravity of my life-change, of my extraordinary leap, of my aloneness and helplessness, all added up into one monumental challenge. I had expertly handled leaving a marriage, finding an apartment, moving, filing divorce papers, all the while working on a design project budgeted at $147 million, but now, this silly shrieking fire alarm seemed to shatter my confidence. The idea that I was all alone and didn't have a partner to turn to for the smallest of handyman tasks in the middle of sleepless nights was inordinately devastating. I sat in shambles on the kitchen floor, drowned in tears.

Then I picked up, changed, drove to a Fred Meyer that I knew was open all night, and bought a step-stool and a 9V battery. I had always refused to climb a step-stool, even on construction sites for interior spaces in which I was sometimes required to do so, because I had serious vertigo, a common companion to migraines. But there I was, at one in the morning, standing on my newly acquired step-stool, unhooking the fire alarm and replacing the battery inside. I sat on my floor-mattress afterwards, hugging my knees in a feeling of quiet triumph. There – I had fixed the fire alarm – *all by myself*. I fell asleep.

Over a year down the road, living in the same condominium complex, but now as a proud homeowner of one of the developer-refurbished one-bedroom units with a view of my faithful guide Mt. Rainier, the fire alarms in the entire building went off. It was Seattle's glorious summertime, and I had recently determined to learn inline skating. When the alarms sent shrill sirens throughout the building, on complete whim, I quickly changed, grabbed my car keys and sped off to Alki beach in West Seattle, with all my gear. I had been out skating only twice before, both times with company and help. The first time I was barely able to stand, the second time all I did was stand. So it wasn't progress that prodded me to go, but just plain, audacious whim.[10]

The moment I stood in the grass adjacent to the trail after parking my car and putting on my gear, I regretted it all. I looked like a fool, standing in one spot, with nowhere to go. My feet were rooted to the ground, my body felt numb, and all I could do was…well, just stand there. Then a little voice inside me said, "Come on baby, you can do it, step out, one foot at a time, come on…" I put one foot forward and immediately slid back. I tried the other and both slid back. I went back and forth, moving ten inches or fewer at a time, all in one spot. Progress!

Then suddenly, I don't quite know what happened. Whether the voice kept urging me, or whether my legs did their own bidding, all of a sudden I was moving, gliding, ever so slowly with the wind. I felt exhilarated and panicked all at once. I went about fifty feet and back like that, like a little girl just having figured out her first fumbling steps, ready to stumble and fall any moment.

Then the angels began to come, one by one. One gal, speeding by gracefully on her blades, cheered me on, saying, "Side-to-side, honey, side-to-side! You're getting it!" I began to sway – side-to-side – and found a bit more motion. Soon after, a guy who had previously whizzed by on his blades like a world champion (making me smile at him nervously and incredibly envious of his flying with the wind), stopped on return and said, "Hi! Having fun?" "I'm Mark," he shook my hand. "I coach many people to rollerblade!" Twenty minutes later, I had completed my first full-on inline skating coaching session.

Mark taught me to move my center of gravity forward with bent knees, and hands splayed to the front. He told me that the most important thing to learn was how to *stop* once I was in motion, and taught me how. He also showed me little exercises I could do on the grass to learn the stopping stance, and to find my balance on each individual foot, with the other lifted off the ground. I exchanged pleasantries with Mark, thanked him from the bottom of my heart, and after he glided away, I resumed my baby steps, this time, practicing how to stop.

Just as I was getting somewhere, a third angel came along. He was on a bike. "Having fun yet?" He too asked. "I am a competitive skater; I could give you some tips!" After

---

10. I had begun to see by then, that inspired whim is not irresponsibility, but the cheerful partner to healthy instincts, and always my prerogative. I made a special effort to practice inspired whim on a regular basis!

recommending different indoor skating locations in the Seattle area and waxing eloquent about the importance of wearing elbow pads, Angel-3 disappeared with the wind. I glided back and forth with the fresh lessons in my head slowly moving into my body. Soon, I was skating about a hundred feet at a time.

In learning to walk all over again, I stumbled and fell, and often grasped at things outside me: substances, objects, people. But gradually, I realized that whether along the waterfront or in life, whether on wheels or off them, my source of power – my center of gravity – is never outside me, but right here within my core. Like Mark had taught me, all I had to do was to remember it, connect with it, and go! [11] And of course, my angels in the Universe would always be there in the right place and at the right time, should I need them!

Cocooning While Reaching:
Aloneness, Not Loneliness

"If you are lonely while you're alone, you are in bad company."

– Jean Paul Sartre

Nature and nurture had colluded, sometimes in contradictory ways, to my developing an acute fear of being alone. I started out being an outgoing, gregarious and extroverted child, preferring the company of adults and their rich complex conversations, rather than the solitary fantasyland that my younger sister seemed to so easily inhabit. (I discovered later that both methods were our coping mechanisms in an unsettling home environment, albeit using our respective inclinations for extraversion and introversion.) As is the case with many extroverts, I preferred to talk out my thoughts with others, rather

---

11. Another year later, I took formal inline skating lessons with a brilliant skater, teacher and mentor, Trish Alexander. Trish disallowed her students from having a helping hand, or from using railings or the walls of the rink at all times, even when losing balance. She insisted – without exception – that we find our balance naturally, and taught us, instead, how to fall safely to the ground!

than relying on an inner world like my sister did.

With a turbulent relationship between my parents, I had developed a fear of abandonment, and therefore, my innate gregariousness had crossed the line into an acute fear of being alone. I was happiest when surrounded by many voices, talking a lot and sharing easily, so much so that my mother often gruffly rebuked me for my gullibility. On top of this, I had coped with my difficult childhood by leveraging my many talents and becoming a high-achiever. Without realizing it, I had turned into somewhat of a pleaser, making my life decisions for the reward of external affirmation. In this way, my otherwise natural and healthy extraversion eventually became exaggerated into a chronic reliance on others' opinions and approval, which was frequently at odds with my fiercely independent intellect and natural leadership qualities.

Stepping on egg shells in over eight years of marriage further hampered any ability to be certain of my own instincts and decisions; I had grown a deeply ingrained belief that everything was my fault. As a result, while my extraversion made me appear to be an open book, I held many a dark secret close to my chest, repressing and internalizing, with severe ramifications.

So, the initial 'coming out' after long years of repression had involved a lot of verbal processing with many, many generous and loving listeners: my therapist Anya, Andrew, Robb, Rachael, my sister Sharmishtha, my parents and best friends back in India, my colleague Scott, my other couple-friends Srivani and Sandeep or Blaine and Heather, my close graduate school friends Bidisha and Tully, and several others. But, once I became aware of my spiritual center of gravity through the example and wisdom of my body, I began to practice connecting with it every time I lost balance, instead of grasping at something or someone outside me.

Because one's center of gravity is seated so deeply within oneself, a corollary of this practice was a growing comfort with utter solitude, not just physical – I was becoming quite accustomed to living and navigating my life alone – but also emotional and spiritual solitude. Over time, by allowing the space for my tears, by listening to my body's pointers, and by connecting with my center of gravity, I experienced less and less need for longer deliberations, not only with others, but also within my own head. I found a greater awareness of and reliance on plain instinct.

One instance of this was my making an offer on the one-bedroom condominium unit in my building, on a warm July night, without discussing it with anyone at all. I wasn't hiding anything; I was simply not feeling the need to voice any deliberations, let alone entertain them even inside my own mind. I was acting on instinct: I just wanted a place of my own. Later, my therapist gently reminded me that people in depression or big transitions like a divorce are generally advised not to make significant decisions, such as investing in property. But I felt quite comfortable and at peace with my instinctive choice.

While I grew into my solitude, my alert instincts also steered me clear of the dangers of social isolation. I discovered that healthy companionship could be sought in collective experiences with perfect strangers: in movie theaters and coffee shops, at the Seattle Art Museum or at the Pike Place Market. The Market, with its sights, smells and sounds, and with throngs of people navigating fish and food and coffee, remotely resembled the density of India on a normal day. I inhaled it all in, watching people, eating small bites, reading a book. All at once, I had both solitude and company.

Whenever I needed them, my angels in the Universe were also still around and available. If my instincts told me it was best to actively seek out familiar company, I invited myself over to close friends' places and hung out in their kitchens and living rooms, participating in their daily family lives, often staying back for a meal. In this process I discovered something lovely and special about American society (which included my assimilated Indian friends): It allowed me solitude and anonymity without reproach; it welcomed me into warm and supportive kitchens and family rooms without demanding obligatory status reports, a tricky, delicate balance.[12] I found that I could just as easily take up an offer at Robb and Rachael's to spend Christmas with them and their boys, as I could choose to be alone over Thanksgiving without much explanation.

I went on to understand that this opening and closing, extending and cocooning, reaching out and reaching in, is what 'managing boundaries' is all about, a totally foreign concept for me, growing up in my turbulent family, and in a strongly communal culture. I began to see the big difference between loneliness and aloneness.

Loneliness is a void, a lack, a dearth of the healthy and necessary social company of others. It is dangerous, and can result in isolation, and even in death! Aloneness, on the

---

12. I often mused that this balance would probably have been hard to achieve in India as a recently divorced young woman going through difficult times, where well-meaning relatives and friends might have swarmed into my life, taking care and taking charge, but who is to know for certain? Ever-evolving India never ceases to surprise me!

other hand, is a comfortable relationship with oneself, and therefore a sign of healthy self-esteem. So, loneliness is a form of disconnection, while aloneness is a form of connection! It can co-exist with companionship; in fact, it is possible (and all right!) to be happily alone in the company of others. Aloneness is incredibly healing and rejuvenating. No matter whether one is an introvert or extrovert, the ability to spend significant amounts of time in one's own company is absolutely essential in the process of centering, finding and maintaining balance.

I believe my instincts; I trust my Higher Power

Centering is the spiritual equivalent of finding my footing. It is an instantaneous reset (or sometimes a process), by remembering and reclaiming my innate ability to look after, nurture and heal myself, a divine gift which is always, already available. It is an unshakeable trust in my own instincts, not threatened by my mind's rationalizations.

Centering in action is:

– Letting go of false personal control, taking the leap of faith, and trusting the Universe (and its angels) to step forward and catch me in its arms;

– Feeling and accepting pain, which is also the first step to freedom from suffering;

– Placing 'matter over mind,' allowing my physical body and all its subtle sensations to guide me, thereby activating an ancient, sophisticated, innate wisdom;

– Connecting fully with my center of gravity, my source of power, which is never outside me, but always right here within my core;

– Cultivating the ability to be joyously and generatively in my own company: a healthy aloneness.

Centering is hardly a stage in a linear path; it is a practice that I find I must attend to on a daily basis, in a more effortful way when I stumble and lose my balance, and at other times as a gentle, constant awareness of my powerful center of gravity.

For David

2.
CONSCIOUSNESS

Consciousness is the awakening to presence; it is the unwavering knowing that *now* is all that I have and all that is real; it is the supreme connection to my soul and to my Higher Power, through my body, and in spite of my mind.

My present is my gift

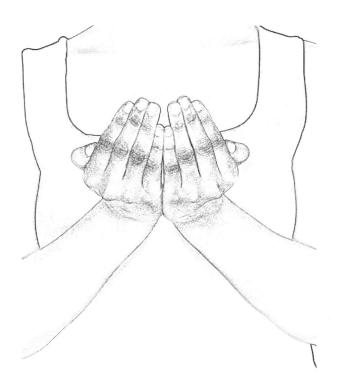

Struggles with Time:
Future Becomes Past without Being Present

"This is the use of memory:
For liberation – not less of love but expanding
Of love beyond desire, and so liberation
From the future as well as the past."

– T.S. Eliot

In those long months of 2005, even in the midst of paralyzing suffering in which I couldn't function or see past two-hour increments, (or perhaps because of it), I began having a hunch – an early awakening of consciousness – that much of my suffering was related to the mind-based concept of linear time, the notion that there is a past, a present and a future.

Time as past was enabled in my mind as memory. I was blessed with an incredible memory for events, and therefore, a long and deep record of the past was ingrained in my brain with a stubborn and unfailing accuracy and dependability, so much so that others could easily use me as their history book or events calendar! With this, came the burden of unforgettable atrocities that I believed I had endured. So, clearly, the attachment to time past was a source of suffering.

Time as future was also tied to my suffering! I had been accustomed to seeing into the future, and was blessed with the ability to be a meticulously planner: plan the next education step or career move, make the next adventurous travel plans or book tickets for a visit to family in India, make sound financial or property investments, plan birthday surprises for loved ones … look forward to this and look forward to that.

But suddenly, all this changed; it was forced out of sheer necessity to change. Looking into the past for even a moment proved so painful that it became physically impossible to do very much. And looking into the future showed me nothing but an empty blackness, so that was equally painful, frightening, and futile. So, other than simply extinguishing myself, the only way to be was to think and act in two-hour increments, the intervals at which the deluges of tears hit.

Each time it felt as if I might not make it through the next two hours, I would simply breathe deeply after all the tears were exhausted, drink a glass of water, and make a short list of things that I needed to accomplish in the next two hours. Then I'd return my attention to the selected activity of the moment. Gradually, something unexpected and magical happened. In those sparingly few moments of focus, I had incredible clarity. With no past and future considerations at play, all extraneous thoughts were put aside, and I did only the work at hand: simply, creatively, imaginatively, and productively.

At the time, I was working on one of the most significant projects The Boeing Company had undertaken: to transform the workplace environment in the factory in which it assembles four of its planes, the 747, 767, 777, and the then soon-to-be launched Dreamliner (787). I had the responsibility of creating a process of organizational discovery, and helping the team translate the findings into a framework for design. In the two-hour increments of work time punctuated with bouts of tears in the mega bathrooms of the Everett Factory, (which is the largest building by volume in the world), I started to have mini strokes of genius.

I began doing what I (and also my firm) recognized later as the best work of my corporate career up to that point! The project became the perfect, fertile landscape for me to find perspective, and bloom creatively. The sheer scale of everything – the factory, the magnificent airplanes, even the gloomy mega bathrooms – all allowed me to stand still and find perspective. My problems, my life-saga and I were so miniscule in that awe-inspiring environment, that they disappeared.

Eventually, I began to recognize that this 'inability' to dwell on the past or plan for the future was actually a newfound *ability* – to remain solely in the present! In fact, I was now incapable of doing it any other way! Initially I had thought that my recent incapacitation for planning, managing and foreseeing would cripple me. Occasionally I had even feared being jobless and homeless.

Instead, the pure and unwavering focus on only *this* moment meant that I had stopped wasting any energy on 'problems' outside my control, such as, a promotion at work that had eluded me for several years, or my drastically reduced standard of living (lowered by more than fifty percent as soon as I stepped out of my marriage). Within the next two years, I was promoted twice, my income increased by forty percent, and the Boeing project won several prestigious firm-wide awards, all without my doing anything outside the moment's calling: *at every moment.*

Although I was technically diagnosed with clinical depression, this became a time of tremendous spiritual awakening and clarity. Often I would wake up in the wee hours of the morning after barely getting three hours of sleep, with strange visions, insights, or simply messages, which, in and of themselves, often didn't make immediate sense. Once I had woken up with the phrase *Limestone Diary* in my head, and eventually I'd gone on to write a poem with that title. Another time, I'd woken up with this statement:

Future becomes past without being present.

The accompanying image was a scene from my childhood. I was on a long-distance train to Kolkata to see my grandparents, the stubby, white-painted mileposts by the tracks whizzing by at superfast speed. I could see each one approaching rapidly from a distance, and then I could see it disappearing speedily into the distance, but I could never really see it clearly and fully when it was at the point directly across from me, nearest to me. I couldn't read it, savor it, know it, or embrace it. In the same way, in most of my life *future had become past without being present!*

As I awoke to consciousness and began having longer and longer durations of presence, the pain did not go away entirely, but eventually, I stopped suffering it. By focusing on just this moment's calling, pain and joy began to appear to me simultaneously. The same feelings that had earlier taken solely the form of pain, took on the simultaneous and paradoxical form of joy.

In these moments, I continued to have visions of divine coded messages everywhere: in an advertisement on a bus, in the local newspaper, in a savings coupon. My angels were also invited in, and little bits of kindness or guidance streamed towards me, showing me what to do next, or which way to turn on the path, exactly in the right ways, and always in the right time: *now*. In these moments of presence, I knew I was not alone, and I knew I was powerful.

The present is indeed…a present. I need look neither forward nor behind!

Obstacles to Consciousness:
Stepping Outside Mind and Time

"The intuitive mind is a sacred gift and the rational mind is a faithful servant. We have created a society that honors the servant and has forgotten the gift."

– Albert Einstein

I had already glimpsed the idea that my suffering is related to the concept of linear time: past and future. Once I had learned to live through my pain in two-hour increments – that is, be fully and uncompromisingly present – I had another unexpected, related insight, this one regarding the relationship between suffering and the mind.

My suffering was rooted in resistance to pain, and in the stories I told myself regarding my pain. But where were these stories coming from? They were generated in my mind due to memory and projections, from the past and into the future, respectively. I saw that these memories, projections and stories, if unguarded and unobserved, eventually add up to so much noise that it can become impossible for me to be present to this moment.

The question then arose: If I have observed this incessant noise-making tendency in myself, *which am I?* Am I the observer, or am I the generator of noise? Who is this observer, who is conscious of, and present to my relentless identification with past memories and future projections? And who is then, the generator of this noise, these identifications, and these attachments? *Which one is the true me?*

Over time, I began having a growing clarity and awareness of these two forces in action. The force that was observing and present felt…well, *soulful*. It was joyous, peaceful, still and empty in spite of everything external, all the chaos, endangerment and suffering I experienced. It was presence itself. Whenever I invoked this presence, my suffering dissolved, even if for fleeting moments. The other force can be best described as…*thoughtful*, that is, full of thoughts, most of the time, obsessively, incessantly, and clingingly so.

The first force, the observer, appears to receive instantaneous strokes of genius, insight, and wisdom, given to it like streaks of light, free gifts from a direct connection with a bigger, more infinite entity, with no intermediaries. Once known, these insights seemed to have always been and always to be; they were independent of past or future. So, I experienced the observer as timeless and formless. I began referring to this force as my soul.

The second force, which I gradually recognized to be my mind, is capable of learning and holding amazing amounts of information, and of conducting incredible analyses. It likes to identify with theories, concepts and beliefs, which it generates as a part of its process. I realized, rather aghast, that in my Indian middle-class values of academic excellence, *this* is what is labeled 'intelligence,' this by-product of mental gymnastics!

Now, I saw that my mind is intended to be a tool for clever operations, subservient to my soul's higher, more intelligent purpose. My mind is the seat of learned knowledge. It is informed, sophisticated and polished: *It is clever but not wise.* It adheres to its learned and glib theoretical frameworks for what is or isn't real, what is or isn't possible, and it needs to process over linear time. My soul, on the other hand, is liberated, and free to venture into the undefined, the uncertain, and the impossible. It is the seat of my imagination and creativity, and it has instantaneous access to eternity.

So, it is my mind that is attached to the concept of linear, sequential time, and it addictively uses the two dimensions in the concept of linear time – the past and the future – to create suffering.

In the first, which is 'before' the present moment in linear time, my mind uses its incredible capacity for memory to continuously recall past events. It then repeats to itself its accounts of these events, and with every repetition, it gives the story a firmer stronghold. Then, it begins to believe that *its story about me is synonymous with the essence of me*, a process of identification. This creates the biggest escape from taking responsibility: Through a persistent narrative that my past is the cause for my present, I can conveniently excuse myself from all accountability!

In the other dimension, which is 'after' the present moment in linear time, my mind makes desperate bids to predict and project what will happen in the future, based on information it believes it has on hand. It aspires to manipulate the future,[13] and is completely

---

13. It is ironic that while the mind believes that it can control the future, it assumes it has no control over the past! A scientist featured in the film *What the *Bleep* do We Know* raises this question in the film, and I paraphrase: Isn't it amazing that we think that by what we do today, we can influence the future, but not the past? Quantum Physics actually has no mathematical framework that says we cannot affect the past!

gripped by this endeavor, making stories about the future as well. This creates the other side of escaping responsibility: Through an obsession with fictitious scenarios in the future, I can avoid appropriate action for the actual situation at hand, in the present moment. Some imagined end, always in the future, begins to justify the means.

Left unobserved and to its own devices, my mind would be addictively and obsessively occupied in this process of analyzing the past and controlling the future. And this would be nothing short of insanity! As this awareness unfolded, I began to organically and effortlessly draw into it, other people's works – writings and speeches – about the same insight. I stumbled upon the writings of Neal Donald Walsch, Eckhart Tolle, and later, Jiddu Krishnamurti, Stephan Bodian, and Gary Zukav. I also began to see new layers of meaning, received not by learning or analysis but by unexpected strokes of light, in the messages of the Bhagvad Gita, and the teachings of The Buddha and Jesus Christ. It was magical! All this collective, resonant insight already in existence began to come into sharp focus and become aligned with my own understanding.

The ability to remain in an awakened state, in which my soul is always in gentle attendance and observation, is consciousness. The term also alludes to a way of being in continuity with other beings, with nature, and ultimately with the infinite, timeless consciousness – the divine – 'Being' in Eckhart Tolle's writings and 'Organism' in Krishnamurti's work.

As I practice consciousness, I often urge myself and my loved ones to step out of the mind, become present, generate a peaceful, loving core, set positive intention, and only then do work or take action. Once, Andrew, also inclined to be cerebral like I've been most of my life, said to me, "I work in my mind. Asking me to get out of my mind is like asking an athlete to get out of his body."

Unlike the mind, however, the body, as I've discovered, is much more in tune with consciousness; it is in fact the path to an awakened state. When I am in attendance to my body and its feelings, I am actually a lot more connected with my soul and my Higher Power, than I can ever be through the workings of my mind. I suspect that the most amazing athletes would say (if they could or wished to articulate this), that they do indeed have to step out of those aspects of body that are ruled by the mind, and then simply connect with their consciousness via an *unthinking* bodily wisdom.

My soul and its consciousness are bigger and higher than my mind or my body, each of which is in service of my soul's creative purpose. If I always work *inside* my mind then how can I *employ* it purposefully? When I live inside my mind, it means I am identified with it. I am fused with it, and cannot separate myself from its delusions, concepts, beliefs, suffering, recorded history, and endless stories. I then falsely, become my mind, instead of being who I really am: my soul and its consciousness, an essential stillness. Left to rule, the mind begins to drive everything I do, and stops serving any real purpose. As the Dalai Lama has said, *"One who is caught in thought loses one's original nature. All he knows are words and descriptions, when he sees the actual thing, he fails to perceive it."*

> With ongoing observation I keep discovering that:
> – My mind is attached to past and future; my consciousness is simply present.
> – My mind makes concepts and beliefs; my consciousness just imagines.
> – My mind talks and thinks; my consciousness listens and perceives.
> – My mind defines and judges; my consciousness explores and observes.
> – My mind controls and preserves; my consciousness liberates and releases.
> – My mind learns and comprehends; my consciousness already knows.
> – My mind likes justice; my consciousness accepts.
> – My mind loves identity; my consciousness doesn't have or need one.
> – My mind is addicted; my consciousness is free.
> – My mind is complicated; my consciousness is simple.
> – My mind moves; my consciousness is still.
> – My mind has sight; my consciousness has vision.

In *The Power of Now*, when Eckhart Tolle uses the term 'unconscious,' he is referring to the state of becoming so fully identified with the mind and its constructs, that one cannot see oneself as separate from the mind. Only upon becoming conscious is one able to step outside and observe the mind, and then employ it appropriately. It is then that it begins to serve one, rather than drive one.

Whenever I am able to achieve this state, even momentarily, I am given those gifts of insight, inspiration and creative visions, which arrive freely and seemingly from nowhere. They come to me not through a laborious, analytical, mental thought-process, but effortlessly and organically through my consciousness. They come as streaks of light and strokes of genius, which are servant to neither time, nor space. We've all experienced such moments, albeit infrequently and fleetingly, when we feel "in the zone," and when "all time stops." There's a way to be like that all the time: It requires constantly stepping outside the mind and observing in consciousness.

Slowing It Down and Allowing Flow:
Cruising on the Road of Life

"Slow down you're doing fine
You can't be everything you want to be
Before your time."

– Billy Joel

In late June of 2006, my childhood best friend from New Delhi, Amrita, finally visited me in Seattle. We had talked about it for years, ever since the inseparable two were separated with my move to America in 1997. But of course it was meant to happen only then: my childhood friend, coming out to share in my rebirth, and to spend time with me in my new home and new life!

As one might imagine, there was much excitement about what all we might do in her twenty-day stay. I wanted, of course, that she spend enough time in glorious, summertime Seattle, and at the same time, I also wanted her to have a taste of the true spirit of America. Being architects and design-lovers, it was tempting to zip around to international design hubs like Chicago, New York, Los Angeles…Or, as I finally proposed to her, we could experience one of America's biggest assets: her natural wonders. And we could do this using her biggest symbol of freedom: the great big automobile!

So, off we went, renting a huge SUV (one-way) for a weeklong road trip along Pacific Highway 101, starting in Seattle and ending in Los Angeles, with various stops in little coast-towns of Washington, Oregon and California, and including larger cities like Portland and San Francisco. (This meant, of course, that Amrita didn't miss out on a good dose of urbanity either.) We stayed in charming bed-and-breakfasts in the various little towns. The changing vegetation, transforming hues of the ocean, and the various sea creatures we saw as we progressed from Oregon to California captivated and mesmerized us.

It was my first time driving such long stretches all by myself; although Amrita is the expert New Delhi driver, it was too complicated to have her drive on the U.S Highway system. A particular stretch of driving became unforgettable for both of us. It is etched into our memories in a way that, to this day, makes us shudder with thrill, and then break into peals of laughter.

Setting off from a little town near Crescent City in northern California, we had arrived at the amazing Redwood National Park, and like the twelve-year-olds we had been when we had first met, we had become so spellbound by the giant, ancient redwood and sequoia trees reaching towards the heavens, and their thick trunks that we could drive right through in our big American SUV, that we did not leave the forest until the late afternoon hours. This was not a smart deviation from the plan, as we were scheduled to cover two-hundred-fifty more miles on twisting-and-turning Highway-101 all the way to San Francisco, and sleep there that night. The next day was The Fourth of July, and we really wanted to feast our eyes on the fireworks over the San Francisco Marina, a first for me too.

As early evening set upon us, we were hungry and tired from all the prancing about in the forest. We stopped for a dinner of fresh seafood, and as soon as the food hit my stomach, my eyelids began feeling heavy. San Francisco was still more than a hundred-fifty miles away, and Amrita gave me a concerned look, saying, "You sure we shouldn't just sleep here and call the motel in San Francisco?" I did stop to think for a moment, but for some reason, San Francisco and the cute brownstone courtyard motel I had booked for us, beckoned to me.

We carried on into the night, and eventually the highway narrowed and began making sharp hairpin turns, the speed limit now lowered to 15mph. The air was becoming a deathly still, the moon had risen high into the sky, and the water below the cliff's edge we were driving on, was a glistening black. It got progressively darker and lonelier, and soon there wasn't a single other vehicle on the road. All I could see at any given moment was the few feet of distance ahead that the SUV's headlights illuminated, and keeping my unwavering eyes on that glowing patch of road, I simply drove on, and on,…and on.

At one moment my eyelids got so droopy that I pulled over and stopped, blinking hard into the stillness. Amrita looked at me nervously, and for a moment I felt fear gripping my stomach. Then I looked up at the moon, and had an impulse to step outside. Amrita followed me, and we stood together, holding hands at America's western cliff-edge, facing the black Pacific Ocean with a full moon over our heads. "Oh my God, this is so beautiful!" she whispered in wonderment and awe. I felt all fear leaving me; I knew my consciousness had returned. I said to her, "Ammu, guess what! If I get too tired to drive, we will become the only two Indian women to sleep in their SUV off Highway 101, facing the Pacific Ocean!" Amrita began giggling in that familiarly delirious way, reminiscent of midnight adventures in the days of our childhood sleepovers, and holding this possibility in mind, we splashed our faces with water and took to the road once again.

The rest of the night followed this pattern. We began to look forward to our stops, to standing outside facing the ocean, smelling the air, splashing our faces with water, and getting on the road again. (Amrita also designed a ceremonious pee-as-you-go program for us: She'd open the two SUV doors on the shoulder-side and instruct me to squat in between the doors, then have me move the vehicle a few feet forward so she had a new spot to decorate!)

On one of our stops, Amrita squealed and then clamped her mouth shut with her palm, pointing into the dark wilderness with her other hand. There were two glittering eyes, reflecting the moonlight. I quickly turned the vehicle's lights on, and we saw a beautiful baby deer staring at us, its deeply lined and vulnerable eyes opened wide. It was a breathtaking sight. At another moment, when we were on one of the hairpin turns, a totally unbelievable sight emerged: a man on a skateboard, gliding smoothly and effortlessly, moving in the opposite direction, like a ghost on wheels! So, we're not the only crazy ones, we said to ourselves.

We sang along with the Bollywood music playing on CDs, took in the invisible ocean and the full moon, and five unbelievably long hours of hairpin turns and 15mph signs later, the road suddenly straightened out, and we knew we were getting somewhere. Before we knew it, the Golden Gate Bridge was upon us. Amrita yelled out a triumphant cry like you wouldn't believe it. "It's the Golden Gate Bridge!!!" She yelled and yelled and yelled. "I have studied it and taught about it, and seen endless photographs of it … and never in my life could I have imagined entering San Francisco over the Golden Gate Bridge at 3 o'clock in the morning!!!"

Since that night, I am never able to look at the full moon and not think of the amazing, wondrous, joyous, free-spirited, exhilarating moments I had with my childhood best friend, driving along the Pacific Ocean. Was that a good plan? Probably not. Would most people advise driving on Highway 101's most treacherous stretch in the middle of the night? Certainly not. Did we get to San Francisco? Yes! Did we have *fun*, the time of our lives? Yes, yes, yes! Not only can I not forget that night, but whenever I have felt remotely low since then, finding the moon in the sky and remembering that night has instantly changed my perspective. It is an unforgettable reminder that I can *always* find my way. All I need is to become present, to remain connected to the now, to remain in consciousness.

Awakening to consciousness to cruise on the road of life is not much different than my free-spirited road trip with Amrita. I become present to the place from where I am starting out, and I make an intention to get to a certain destination. (I could even start out saying that I cannot name my destination, but that I know I want to head southward to a beautiful place, and I want to experience the ocean along the way.) Once I have set the intention for my destination, I have absolutely nothing else of long-term concern to focus on. My headlights illuminate two-hundred feet at a time, and all I need to do is to make sure I pay attention to what I can see, and stay on the road.

Every now and again, a sign shows up, and since I know my destination, I will have learned to read the signs correctly, and take the correct arm in every fork in the road. Sometimes I encounter roadblocks, but if I pay attention, I will find signs for a detour. Sometimes I inadvertently make a mistake and take a wrong turn, but if I am calm and patient with myself, and remember my destination, I will find my way again with the help of a local or map or other posted signs. Nowhere on a long-distance road-trip can I see the entire roadway I am about to take, and never can I really know how I'll get from where I am to where I want to go. Sometimes there are milestones that inform me where I am relative to my destination, and at other times, there are none.

Consciousness is made possible by continuously practicing presence in this way: setting intentions, keeping my eyes intently on the next two hundred feet that I can see, and reading the signs, the instant messages, the streaks of light gifted by my Higher Power. When I am present, have the highest and best intention, and have feelings of joy, then the signs from my Higher Power become clearly visible, recognizable and actionable. I do not get lost, and when I take detours it is because there are better sights to delight in along the way! When I am in tune with my intention and my intention is in tune with the Universe, then there is simply not an iota of doubt that I will get to a desired future!

Over-informed, Hyper-busy, and Multi-tasking:
Arjuna and the Fish Eye

"To allow oneself to be carried away by a multitude of conflicting concerns, to surrender to too many demands, to commit oneself to too many projects, to want to help everyone in everything, is to succumb to the violence of our times."

– Thomas Merton

A little story from the Hindu epic, *The Mahabharata*, about the renowned master Dronacharya training the Pandava brothers in the art and skill of archery, is firmly etched into my childhood memory of Indian mythology. It goes thus. Once, the five Pandava brothers and their estranged sixth brother Karna were assembled for a lesson with Guru Drona, and he tied a wooden fish high on a tree above a pool of water. He then asked each student, one by one, to take the archer's stance, instructing them to aim their bow and arrow at the fish's eye, while gazing only at its reflection in the water below.

As each student came along and took his turn, Guru Drona made them pause in the stance and asked, "Son, what all do you see?" The oldest, Yudhisthira, answered, "The sky, the tree, the …," and before he could finish, Drona stopped him and replaced him with the next boy. Faced with the same question, Bhima answered, "The branch of the tree, the fish, the…," and met the same fate. Even Karna, arch rival to Arjuna, was stopped and asked to step aside. When Arjuna the ace-archer stepped up, he answered without hesitation or equivocation, "I see the eye of the fish." And Guru Drona exclaimed with delight, "Shoot!"Arjuna's arrow shot unwaveringly out of his bow, and pierced right through the eye of the fish.

One of the biggest obstacles to being fully present and allowing our consciousness to lead us, is our cultural, mass-scale obsession with what I like to call 'more and instant.' More stuff, more food, more information, more news, more Facebook friends, and all just now! We are frequently impressed and awed by people who are very informed, hyper-busy, have little time, and multi-task constantly. "Wow," we think to ourselves, "she must be important!"

With globalization and forever evolving technology, we are now essentially overcome with having and knowing more, and having it easily, instantaneously, simultaneously and incessantly. We are so busy that there is no time for doing things that really matter. We're so over-informed that we don't know what's truly relevant. We're so over-stimulated that we cannot fully feel. And we're doing so many things at once that we're not doing anything at all. Speaker, entrepreneur and author of Your Business Brickyard Howard Mann wrote in a blog post:

"…The echo chamber we're building is getting larger and louder. More megaphones don't equal a better dialogue. We've become slaves to our mobile devices and the glow of our screens … We walk the streets with our heads down staring into 3-inch screens while the world whisks by doing the same. And yet we're convinced we are more connected to each other than ever before. Multi-tasking has become a badge of honor. I want to know why…"

As an architect, Mies van der Rohe's timeless reminder that "less is more" had molded and shaped my design sensibilities from an early age. What about my attitude and conduct in my everyday life, however?

One particular repetitive experience, when working in the large, global design firm, proved insightful in this regard. As a human-centered design strategist, I was focused on clients and their organizational world with considerable breadth and depth. So, quickly, I became a strategic contributor in marketing, in interviewing and 'winning' work for the firm. As in any industry, preparing for a job interview in order to land a big contract was always a highly strategic, competitive and high-pressure affair. The primary team sat with a host of advisors and experts in a closed room for hours on end, sometimes over three to five days, brainstorming, pinning up ideas on index cards, and shaping, honing and rehearsing a message.

A senior managing partner, Scott, was almost always found as a coach in the room (if he wasn't already part of the actual interviewing team). Scott was a quick study, a brilliant strategist, and an utterly charming salesperson. He taught us to be thorough in our research: to inquire into every single aspect of the client and their enterprise. He showed the team how to hone a precise message and build confidence in "asking for the job." "Why should they hire you?" he asked with a fiery energy, making us answer the question repeatedly till we got it right. "Think in terms of benefits, not features!" he often reprimanded us. Unlike some others who were exhausted by this process, I was always energized by it. I thoroughly enjoyed and looked forward to these sessions with Scott, as I did to taking my lessons from him to client interviews.

One of the other activities Scott emphasized was to learn everything we could about the competition in the fray. Who are they? What are their strengths? What do we offer that they don't, on account of which we might outshine them? In my early years learning to strategize and win projects, and as an ardent fan of Scott's, I had followed his guidance to the letter.

Once I began to access consciousness, however, I began to see the fallacy of information, something I had so enjoyed all my life as a mind-centric person. I saw that there was a pretty early point by which we became over-informed and thereby, de-focused and distracted from that which is really important and relevant. At the level of driving outcomes, I observed that by focusing on details such as competitors' qualifications and shortcomings, we were crafting 'winning' sales messages which scored us work, but most of it only a reasonable if not poor fit with the team's real passion and skills, because we were leading with differentiation with competitors instead of with the purity of what we loved and were good at doing. Being stuck with unloved or half-loved projects for three to seven years is like winning battles but losing a long, arduous war! All we needed to do was to talk about what we loved, with love!

It was at this juncture that I accessed fresh insight from the story of Arjuna and the Fish Eye. I began to train myself to look only at the eye of the fish, each time, every time. I noticed how tempting it was to study the sky, the tree, and the birds. I observed how we collectively, more often than not, looked everywhere but there, convincing ourselves that we were working hard, learning more, doing better…when all we did was foster an illusion of being gainfully busy.

On one such marketing pursuit for the Los Angeles International Airport's expansion, I dared to digress from the high-pressure preparation at hand, and took the time to relate Arjuna's story to two senior gentlemen on the project, one of whom was Japanese. I still recall the look in his eyes; it was as if a lesson from one ancient culture had struck a deeply resonant chord with a person from another ancient culture. He came to my desk later in the day to personally thank me for becoming an important leader in the firm!

While our consciousness is at peace with uncertainty and enjoys a deeper, more innate knowing, our minds always want to gather more superficial information, mainly so that they can predict, shape and control outcomes. This focus on outcomes – also an important subject in *The Bhagvad Gita* within the epic *Mahabharata* – may be why it has been believed that information is power. But the real impact of most information is the creation of a tremendous amount of noise, on which our minds love to feast and obsess, and a resulting loss of authentic power. Two important and related illusions are propagated:

– The first illusion is that we have an acute shortage of time.
– The related illusion is that life is terribly, inordinately busy.

Our minds, obsessed with information, buy into the fallacies of less time and more busyness. They become crippled with the limitations they perceive, multi-tasking their way into 'success.' And when they win, they win for the wrong reasons, winning the battle but ultimately, losing the war.

Focusing on the eye of the fish allows us to edit irrelevant information and harness the timeless moment, what some have called the Eternal Now. Focusing on the eye of the fish enables us to be present. Time expands to allow the needful to happen, for truth to reveal itself. Many athletes jumping to great heights, or people in life-and-death situations will tell you how "time stood still" when they took their one and only shot. Our consciousness is always naturally tuned into these constraint-free, timeless moments of truth and true knowing. We simply have to get out of its way.

Practicing Presence:
Being a Traveler, Not a Tourist

"The traveler sees what he sees, the tourist sees what he has come to see."

– G.K. Chesterton

In the years after I was forced to become present, I recognized that what was awakened as a latent ability in a time of life-threatening crisis must now be intentionally accessed and continuously practiced. With 'normality' gradually returning to my life, it had become easy to get caught up in the next cause for suffering, in the *maya* (illusion) of control of the future, or in *moha* (attachment) to the joys or sorrows of the past. The present moment is frequently lost in the greedy bid for the future, or the nostalgic attachment to the past. This moment – the only one we can really experience at any instant, the only one we can truthfully know, and the only one we can influence – ruefully slips through our fingers.

The biggest obstacle to practicing presence is becoming distracted with 'planning for the future,' for the destination. We become tourists, wanting to get somewhere that is already on the map. Most of us struggle with objections and questions like: But how can I ensure that the best things will happen in the future if I am always only responding to the present? What should be my short-term actions, and what should be my long-term actions? Businesses, in particular, appear to be spending hours on end of high-value time trying to forecast, strategize and plan, and many individuals and couples take similar approaches to their lives, for aspects such as their relationship, finances, career, and parenthood.

My personal conviction is that if I do what is highest and best in this moment – the only moment I really have – the best things will automatically happen in my future. So, what is the 'highest and best' response in this moment? For me, it is one that:
- Requires pure, unfettered love towards both myself and others;
- Challenges me to extend and grow at the level of my soul-purpose, beyond the comfort zone of my mind, and
- Is completely free of all attachment to any imagined future scenarios or out comes.

My access to presence was deepened by three concerted practices: traveling, Vipassana meditation, and unconditional love!

Whether on a holiday journey or life journey, one can adopt one of two roles: tourist or traveler. As a tourist, one is primarily focused on the destination, on 'getting somewhere.' Milestones are mapped out: the Major Museum, the Ancient Monument, the Best Restaurant, the Famous Lake, the Tallest Mountain. The time in between getting to these wonderful places is an interval to recuperate from the last destination, and then plan and set out for the next; thus there is a sense of alternating highs and lows. Total time at a Major Destination is sub-divided into several of these important Mini-Destinations, and it is ensured that one makes it to all or most of these, or the trip may not be deemed successful. Thus, there is a sense of urgency, and also a definition of success or a 'good time' associated with this type of venture.

As a traveler, one is primarily focused on the journey: on where I am now. There are points of arrival in the sequence that one notices with pleasure and joy, but no distinct destinations. One does not have to get anywhere but just here, *where one already is*. An inner compass of 'what do I feel like now?' guides the journey, without map or timetable, but nevertheless, an innate and resonant sense of timing. The Major Museum, the Ancient Monument, the Best Restaurant, the Famous Lake and the Tallest Mountain may or may not come by, and if they do, they are noticed, appreciated and celebrated. Also come along the humble shack, the tiny bug, the elaborate flower, the messy cloud, and the unexpected river. Weaving in and out of things expected and unexpected, the senses are heightened to experience everything. There are no good or bad associations, no important or unimportant things, no great or terrible weather, no hard-lined definitions of success. Every moment is experienced as equally precious and every find as equally miraculous.

It is easy to see how physical journeying is a great metaphor for life itself. In life too, we can be tourists, or we can be travelers. In life too, it is easy to get caught up in destinations, with the times in between simply becoming instruments to plot the next this or that. Whether one is learning a new skill or picking up a new language, dating (or married, for that matter), working in a job, practicing music, deepening one's yoga practice … it's all too easy to become preoccupied with the milestones and major destinations, instead of enjoying the journey itself.

In a Vinyasa Yoga class one night, I was struggling to get into a difficult *asana*, becoming annoyed and disappointed at my 'failure,' when the instructor's voice rang through the studio: "It's easy to forget what you're *really* doing here: You're breathing, remember? You're busy being alive." What a great reminder to gently nudge me back into the journey!

In practicing presence, my body has repeatedly served as the missing link. In mid-2008, I hit a new crisis point with my work life – an unbearable ennui, a definite sense of not belonging in the corporate machine – although I didn't know yet where I wanted to go instead. It was time for the next layers of false self to fall away and reveal a deeper authenticity. With a suspicious punctuality, the Universe conspired once again and began sending me messages, this time about Vipassana meditation. My friend and colleague Scott told me about his experience with it over the years, and another colleague Cathy was considering taking a leave-of-absence and attending a Vipassana course. Other literature began coming my way, and by August that year, I had signed up for a rigorous ten-day course at the Northwest Vipassana Center.

So there I was, in the small town of Onalaska, at the border of Washington and Oregon, relinquishing my wallet, car keys, photographs, speech, and all human interaction, for ten long days of sitting still on a meditation pillow and observing my body's sensations! Vipassana gifted me with a two-thousand-year-old methodology of remaining present simply by observing breath and body, and practicing it has profoundly shaped my course since. I turned permanently into a traveler.

The ultimate cultivation of presence, however, has been the practice of unconditional love. To love is such a simple thing, such a deep thing, such a natural thing, such a universal thing… yet how difficult it is to do without focusing on milestones and destinations!

I received the immense gift of this challenge in the opportunity to unconditionally love my twin soul, Andrew. When I first experienced my purer nature, my highest potential reflected in the mirror, it was so easy to become attached to that powerful and moving experience, and to saddle it with expectations, guarantees and outcomes. When I relinquished these tourist-like destinations and instead, dedicated myself to being a traveler – exploring and honoring my creative potential that was revealed through our loving interactions, and understanding my wholeness within myself – I was able to truly love Andrew, *just* to love him. Loving unconditionally became the epitome of being present, the ultimate practice of consciousness.

As The Mother of Sri Aurobindo Society has said: *"At first, one loves only when one is loved. Next, one loves spontaneously, but one wants to be loved in return. Then one loves even if one is not loved, but one still wants one's love to be accepted. And finally one loves purely and simply, without any other need or joy than that of loving."*

I used to be a tourist, both on holidays and in life…and in love. The next degree, the next job, the next move, the next recognition, and all the mapping, planning and organizing in-between; how I had reveled and excelled in that! But the little room that way of being gave me to grow in unexpected directions, to welcome the serendipitous, or to discover alternative paths, made it utterly claustrophobic to live that way. When I (wryly) contemplate the ultimate 'destination' as we know it in flesh-and-blood – physical death – it becomes quite clear that focusing on the destination doesn't get us anywhere!

Today, I am a traveler, both in my physical journeys and in love and life, harnessing the power of the Eternal Now. Every time I encounter a milestone, I celebrate it, and then

I return to the path of simply being in the journey. I've come to see that:

- The means *is* the end!
- The process *is* the product!
- The journey *is* the destination!

My present is my gift

Consciousness is the state of being present, characterized by an unwavering knowing that *now* is all I have and all that is real. It is a connection to my soul, through my body, and in spite of my mind.

Consciousness in action is:

– Relinquishing linear time in the form or past or future, and recognizing that the present is all there is;

– Awakening to my soul's ability to observe the mind and employ it appropriately in the purpose of the soul;

– Slowing down to allow divine flow: setting intentions and reading the signs, the instant messages, the streaks of light freely gifted from my Higher Power;

– Dispensing with addiction to all extraneous information and focusing on absolutely nothing but the highest and best action of the moment;

– Being a traveler not a tourist, needing to be nowhere but just here, where I already am.

By definition, consciousness is not an end-state that can be achieved, or a destination that can be reached. It is a constant, moment-to-moment practice. At every turn, the mind, ego and constructs of linear time take over, but in every instance that I have awareness of this inclination through the eternal observer – my soul – I am in consciousness. In these moments I have absolute clarity, stillness, timelessness, love and peace. Thriving is about accessing these moments more and more consistently, so that they become a way of being.

For Sharmishtha

3.
COMPASSION

Compassion is my connection to the loving, benevolent, and forgiving quality of the Universe, resulting in the cultivation of the same within me, opening my heart to pure, essential love for others, always including myself. Without implying reconciliation or co-dependence with toxic people and situations, compassion is an intentional, energetic response of love toward them, activating true healing and authentic power.

In forgiveness is my freedom

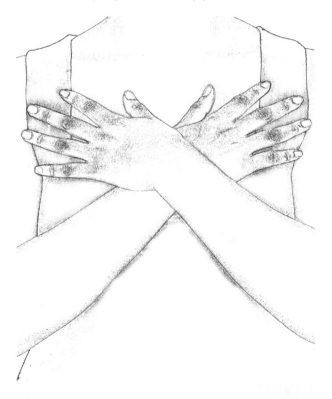

Becoming Powerless to Regain Power:
Let Go and Let God

"Control is never achieved when sought after directly. It is the surprising outcome of letting go."

– James Arthur Ray

To this day, I reflect with gratitude, wonderment and sheer awe upon the immense kindness and open-heartedness I received in those early years of stumbling and learning to walk all over again. And really, it has never stopped coming my way since, particularly when I let go and remain in consciousness. What compelled all these people – family, friends, acquaintances, strangers – to do the things they did for me? How did they magically appear, exactly when I needed them, and in the ways I needed them? How did I get so many free gifts?

I still marvel at Robb's words to me, sitting in a tiny Vietnamese restaurant in Seattle's International District, when I'd protested, "But you can't take me home just like that! You hardly know me...and Rachael hasn't even met me yet!" Rolling his eyes in mock frustration, he'd said, in what I learned over time to be his characteristically smart-ass way, "Hey, all we've been hearing about for a couple of years is Shahana-this and Shahana-that, including all about your fabulous cooking. I'm only helping you because I want Indian food for life." Then he'd added somewhat solemnly, "Clearly Andrew loves you and we love Andrew, so we already love you too."

The transitive property of love! Really? Could it be just *that simple*? Could it really be that I could just let go, and know that there would always be open, loving arms to catch me?

Well, yes. It *is* that simple. By my letting go of control and trusting my Higher Power, I found that the Universe was able to guide me with signposts and angels in positive, empowered directions. The more I let go, the more I leaped in faith, and the more I lived in consciousness, the greater was my access to the Universe's incredible, unlimited, freely given compassion. Free gifts kept coming my way from several unexpected quarters. I developed a growing faith that the Universe is always here to give me all sorts of caring exactly when and how I need it. *I didn't have to be in charge!*

Most of us, whether we have been in challenging life situations or not, have a significant need for personal control.[14] The need to be in charge, to predict and control outcomes, is linked with our innate instincts for survival – an effort to prevent death – and a chunk of our brains is dedicated to this effort. This is what has been called the 'flight or fight' instinct in the face of perceived danger. The tricky thing as I discovered later, is that this ancient, faithful instinct doesn't quite distinguish between a turbulent family environment and a hungry tiger's salivating mouth! And so it often rages out of control, outstepping its dedicated role and working overtime: to save, to prevent 'death.'

And so it had been with me. As a little child exposed to frequent, turbulent family upheaval, in which fleeing to an alternative place of safety and comfort hadn't been an option, staying to 'fight' appeared to be the way to survive. So, I had played the savior role in my family: I had developed an illusory self-concept of being in charge and in control, of being the 'big girl' who was responsible for my family's well-being, and somehow can make it all okay.[15]

Later, as a young adult, I habitually continued to stay to fight: for my survival, for my marriage, for my then husband, for our families, and so on. Feeding a dangerous cycle, my false belief of control had actually kept me trapped in various damaging situations. In the case of my dysfunctional marriage, I had firmly believed that I could just 'work hard' to salvage it, a survival instinct. This is what Melody Beattie and others have called co-dependence: My need to 'save' was as strong as my partner's need to 'be saved.' This matching need ensured a continuing co-dependence between us, giving sustained life to destructive behaviors and actions.

In Beattie's writings, I came across the phrase, *Let Go and Let God*. These words struck me like an illuminating bolt of lightning because of their strong resonance with my own fresh discoveries. What could easily sound like a cliché from a Ten Steps program or religious doctrine, had intense meaning for me. Now I saw that 'Let God' simply meant allowing my Higher Power, which always knows best, to give me direction. All I needed to do was to be still, and encourage my false, illusory, controlling self to step out of the way.

---

14. For those of us who have experienced prolonged periods of trauma, the tendency to hold on to control can be extreme. For me, it used to manifest as perfectionism, sometimes in the most mundane of things, such as excessive cleaning and tidying to keep my home environment in exemplary order, planning everything in tremendous detail, and so on.
15. I went on to understand that this phenomenon is universal. All of us as little children, even in 'typical' or 'normal' childhood circumstances, create self-images based on early life experiences. These, then, direct the patterns of our adult lives and keep us in 'survival' mode, unless and until this early self-image is dismantled and its patterns disrupted.

Emerging from a long-ingrained pattern of control and co-dependence was not easy, but the process began naturally once I left the marriage, through my body, and its progressive release of previously unexpressed pain. Initially, it appeared as if letting go of control is equivalent to becoming powerless. But like most truths in life, I began to discover that this relationship is also paradoxical: The more control I relinquished, the more authentic power I could actually harness.

Not only had control and co-dependence previously prevented my harmful situation from being positively transformed, they had also obstructed the Universe's abundant compassion, the kind I had now begun to experience, from entering my life. So, by letting go, I had *let God* (help me help myself). Now, instead of swimming upstream in torrential waters and 'winning' against all odds, the right things were beginning to reveal themselves with relative ease, and I was able to flow powerfully in union with them. In this way, becoming powerless allowed me to regain my (Higher) power!

As my knowing and trust deepened in a strongly benevolent and loving Universe, I succeeded in shedding layer upon layer of control, and began instead, connecting with a sea of compassion within myself. I felt an incredible opening of benevolent love towards myself, towards my situation, towards others, and yes, also towards my ex-husband.

The Liberation in Forgiveness:
Why on Earth Should I (Not) Forgive?

"To forgive is to set a prisoner free and discover that the prisoner was you."

– Lewis B. Smedes

Even in the throes of marital discord turned grossly violent, I remember recognizing a look of sheer terror in my then husband's eyes, as he acted out his rage. At the time I didn't have any theoretical knowledge about violence and its patterns, but through this raw, instinctual, in-the-moment observation, I had an insight even then, that the violence I was experiencing and witnessing was really, a terrified inner-child acting out. Since I was still co-dependent, I remained the savior and the hero, pitying his terror and even finding false power in it, and avoiding connecting with the heinous damage being caused to both of us, and especially to my body and my spirit. Survival – staying to 'fight' for 'success' – had also become the source of my victimhood!

After I had broken away, dismantled my co-dependence, and begun healing through the post-traumatic stress disorder, that look of hapless terror in my ex-husband's eyes returned to me time and again. Recalling that inner child's terror in the light of the Universe's compassion that I was being showered with, had an incredible impact on me, for which I am grateful for to this day. It catapulted me almost instantaneously into a place of compassionate forgiveness, and down the road, into a peaceful state of complete acceptance.

The state of compassionate forgiveness that I was now experiencing, was very different from my previous state of co-dependence that had involved pitying, being in control, heroic saving and self-sacrifice. This new state didn't come at my own cost – it was not a zero-sum game – if anything, it was to my benefit, because every drop of compassion I harnessed from the Universe and radiated back, was directed as much towards myself, as it was towards my ex-husband. It had nothing to do with justice and right or wrong, it didn't imply reconciliation, and it certainly didn't involve harboring illusions about my ex-husband, myself, or our relationship. If anything, it allowed me to see everything with a gentle, strong and crystal-clear clarity.

Many consider it downright absurd to actively generate feelings of love and compassion in situations of egregious wrongdoing or harm. "People who act with such cruelty don't deserve a drop of compassion!" they might proclaim self-righteously. "Why would you feel any tenderness or love towards someone who has scarred you emotionally and physically?" they might ask, incredulously. They may even consider it a form of defending, justifying or enabling hurtful and damaging behaviors.

I discovered, however, that the difference between co-dependence and compassion is a rather big one. Co-dependence is an unhealthy state of mutual need that perpetuates negative and harmful behaviors. Compassion is not a need; it is a gift, given freely by choice. It doesn't cost oneself anything, but in fact, it serves both oneself and others.

Through the time that I processed layer upon layer of my own anger, hurt, grief and terror, the compassionate forgiveness I had been fortunate enough to access, stayed with me as a faithful companion and provider of perspective. While I experienced anger and grief, which are necessary and healthy responses to boundary violations, compassion towards my ex-husband protected me from bitterness and resentment, which are like virulent cancers that can consume and eventually kill one's being. They are destructive because they prevent healing and exacerbate the damage already experienced. Further, they harbor a temperament that attracts new, damaging influences into one's life, creating a perpetual cycle of negativity! Bitterness and resentment are serious impediments to a thriving life, and their only antidotes are compassion and forgiveness.

In spite of forgiveness having such a clear and immense personal benefit, why do most of us struggle with it? For one, a common error is to unconsciously confuse forgiveness with concepts of justice, of right and wrong. My discovery showed me that compassion and forgiveness are our prerogative, our uniquely human choice, to be exercised over and above the reasoning of right and wrong. And again, the tremendous benefit of exercising this choice is that it is, ultimately, empowering. Compassion and forgiveness are liberating gifts to oneself, even if given 'undeservedly' to the 'wrongdoers' in our lives.

As I alluded to earlier, the other false belief that causes resistance is that compassion and forgiveness necessarily result in a zero-sum game. Feeling another's pain and forgiving their hurtful actions do not necessarily invalidate or compromise one's own pain, grief, anger or sense of violation. Quite to the contrary, I discovered that by holding compassion and forgiveness in my heart, it was actually easier for me to treat myself with caring and tenderness as well! And surprising as it might sound, I also discovered that along with forgiving others, I eventually needed to forgive myself too: for not seeing it coming or for seeing it coming, for staying or for leaving, for being angry or for not being angry enough, for my own hurtful words and actions in the toxic dynamic…the list is long and complex.

Compassion is an active, energetic state of being, like the sun's radiant, warm, healing and empowering energy. And in radiating it freely towards others we actually end up directing most of it to ourselves. We're embalmed by its warm, regenerative powers. Compassion and forgiveness not only disabled dangerous impediments such as bitterness and resentment, they actually aided and hastened my healing towards a thriving life. So the question was no longer, "Why should I forgive?" but, "Why would I *not* forgive?"

When Being Wronged Becomes Identity:
The Cost of Being Right

"Change in society is of secondary importance; that will come about naturally, inevitably, when you as a human being bring about the change in yourself."

– Jiddu Krishnamurti

Gandhian idealism was one of the most profound influences in my early life, and in later years, it translated into idealistic notions of social and other arenas of justice. I developed a strong identification with concepts of 'rightness' and 'justness,' which was further sealed due to my challenging life experiences.

Abusive circumstances, the antithesis of justness, foster a strange paradox. On the one hand, one's self-esteem, boundaries and sense of right and wrong are diminished, and self-loathing, self-blame and co-dependence can keep one captive in the toxic dynamic. On the other hand, one's sense of rightness (from being egregiously wronged and violated) takes a major stronghold to protect one from complete annihilation. This sense of rightness, initially developed as an inner defense mechanism for survival, can eventually become a driving component of one's external identity and way of being in the world. Suddenly one is a 'Survivor,' and everyone celebrates one's 'Survival.'

So, in spite of my early, fortuitous connection with compassion and forgiveness, I hit a new block down the road of actual practice. I still carried around a self-concept of 'being wronged' in a couple of prominent areas of my life: in the corporate workplace (in the competitive and political environment of which I believed I was being wronged, slighted and out-maneuvered), and in my early childhood memories with my parents. Something told me even in the moment that this wasn't serving me in the least. But I was holding on, because letting go of the 'survivor' identity risked invalidating everything I had endured; it risked the loss of *justice*, for Pete's sake!

Then something happened in the corporate workplace itself, to dislodge my righteousness. A new employee was assigned to the desk next to mine in the open-office system. I learned through the grapevine that Pat was an interior designer with several years of experience, and had come from another well-known, local powerhouse. She was an inscrutable

56

sixty years of age, pranced around with surprising energy in shimmery ponchos, and held her head cocked at an angle. I hadn't made up my mind yet about whether I liked her or not; she seemed a bit strange. But she took to chatting with me with alacrity, and we formed an unlikely friendship.

One day Pat caught me by surprise by making an astute observation about one of the principals in the office, commenting on his unjust actions in good humor, without any emotional charge. The comment promptly ignited a bristling righteousness in me. "Oh, that behavior is simply unacceptable. It makes me so angry!" I exclaimed. "I am passionate about rightness...about justice!" I informed her with vehemence "That's a tough choice," my new neighbor said slowly and deliberately, with a small smile. At my flummoxed expression, she added, "That was exactly my expression when a saintly person once said the same thing to me over thirty years ago."

I was left mulling over my colleague's comment for weeks, if not months. What did she mean by "that's a tough choice"? Is standing uncompromisingly for correctness, rightness, justice, a matter of *choice*? Doesn't everyone naturally favor justice, the right thing? I simply couldn't make any sense of it. Some time later, when the struggle with the comment had left my analytical mind, quite unexpectedly, I spotted a bumper sticker that read: *You can be right, or you can be happy.* This is, of course, a commonplace aphorism, but it was as if I was seeing it for the first time. A powerful insight hit home. My neighbor's comment from a few months ago fell right into place, without the thoughtful analysis or ruminations that had previously led me nowhere.

I realized that doing right and living in integrity have nothing to do with 'fighting for what's right' in all situations. Fighting in this way is, really, an effort to control (via opposition) what one judges and labels as the negative, 'wrong' force. And such control is nothing but a mirror image of the control that the alleged negative force is exerting in the first place. By resisting control with control, negativity is empowered and escalated. In an effort to be right, we become wrong. And in this process, we also become unhappy and lose our peace. In being right, critical, and unforgiving, we sacrifice our peace and happiness!

Following my epiphany I began to see many things differently. I observed how, many a violated person wears her (unarguable) rightness both as a shield and as a badge of honor, fighting self-righteously in movements of anti-oppression, anti-violence, anti-war, and other socially 'just' causes. Undoubtedly, I too had carried this attitude into the workplace.

Wonderful and well-intentioned people become so passionate about their cause and so intoxicated by their rightness that they have little or no awareness of how much their true happiness is being compromised. They end up causing drama, inadvertently alienating positive experiences along the way and worse still, reinforcing and manifesting their "I've been wronged" story over and over again. People get so busy being right, that nobody is happy. The activist world is rife with this phenomenon. With anti-this and anti-that, we've become so impassioned and vehement about what we are against that we are often unable to identify what we are *for*: a 'for' that is not defined in terms of an opposition to something else.[16]

So, why do we love to be right? Why must we adhere to our sense of rightness even at immense cost? Why are we so attached to justness; why are we incapable of accepting the grayness of right and wrong?

I've come to see that our attachment to rightness is rooted in a deeper block against forgiveness and healing: The unconscious, inner-child, quite perversely, *does not want to heal*! Now, why in the world would that be? It's because this inner child is afraid of joy, afraid of painlessness. It has been so conditioned by negativity that it clings to its habitual and familiar state of grief and pain, as its means of survival in this world. Giving up the pain would mean the death and annihilation of a significant identity, the identity of a wronged, valiant survivor. Besides, if we're not able to hold others accountable for our pain, then we cannot feel superior, better or bigger, and we may be forced to see our own nakedness and frailties. We may be forced, God forbid, to take responsibility!

So, holding on to a position of rightness becomes necessary in order to avoid the death of a significant identity. This death, of course, would only be of a 'false' self, and it is absolutely necessary to die in this way to *truly* live, to thrive. Holding on to an identity of being wronged, of being a survivor, can have major costs: It can cost us our true life and our true self![17]

As I saw all of this, my self-concept of being egregiously wronged quickly began to shift, transform and eventually, disintegrate. I began finding that in more and more situations, I was less attached to the right thing or to being right (even if I was morally correct!),

---

16. Even when we are vehemently anti-war, we actually energize war as a phenomenon, and thus, perpetuate it!
17. Surviving, thus, competes with thriving, a staggering insight that came up repeatedly in my journey, and does so also in this book. Surviving is antithetic to joyful thriving!

and more capable of simply observing the erroneous actions of others without making them about me or my story. Eventually, my view of my childhood began to transform as well, and I began to see my childhood experiences as my assets rather than as my limitations.

This deeper realization about false identity radically transformed my entire worldview. Now, whenever I catch myself deciding that someone is being bad, wrong, unfair, irresponsible, lazy, oppressive, abusive, criminal...whatever it is, I observe my judgment, then take a deep breath and switch to examining the contexts in my own life in which I might, even remotely, harbor similar tendencies. I assure you, it is an instantly humbling experience: If I am brutally honest, for every misstep of another I witness, I find a shade or shadow of the same lurking somewhere within me. So, every failure of someone else can be used as an opportunity to turn the gaze inward, not critically but compassionately, and thus instantly find compassion for the other, however heinous her erroneous actions may be. And the instant I connect with compassion, I also connect with peace, joy and love.

To be compassionate in this way is not to condone or perpetuate injustice. I've been amazed to discover that accessing compassion and making inner changes in myself can actually be much more transformative in the world than 'fighting' for a cause. This is the true meaning of Mahatma Gandhi's exaltation to us: *Be the change you wish to see in the world.* This is what the Sufis have called the true, greater *jihad*.[18]

In 2007, in the first longer-term relationship I entered since the ending of my marriage, I made an intention of practicing compassionate love. My mantra about my partner became: *Jason is always right.* The true meaning of this ridiculous-sounding statement is that even when he is 'wrong,' there is something in his 'wrongness' that can reveal the right path. I frequently joked with Jason that he can be right so that I can be happy, and this declaration in terms of a trade never failed to make him laugh.

Every time I forgot this simple rule, I was overcome with unhappiness in the relationship. I experienced how lonely it is to cling to one's rightness: One is left hugging one's position or opinion, rather than one's partner! And every time I turned around to his being

---

18. The word *jihad* derives from the Arabic root *jhd*, signifying intense struggle or effort, and therefore it carries the connotations of a moral endeavor directed toward one's own inner improvement, which the Sufis and other eminent Muslims have been quoted as calling *jihad-e-akbar*, or greater *jihad*.

'right,' peace and joy returned to me promptly. How? Because whenever I relinquished my rightness, my partner automatically returned the favor, to join me in a common place of peace, joy and love. (Take my word for it: No one wants to be left hugging nothing but his rightness!) In mature, healthy relationships, this makes space for two people to have the *real* conversation they need to have, rather than struggle with an impasse made of two 'right' perspectives.

So, yes, there *is* a choice: You can be right, or you can be happy. If only small families and big tribes, small associations and big countries alike would access this simple little secret!

The Nature of Acceptance:
Beyond Rightness

"Forgiveness is to offer no resistance to life - to allow life to live through you."

– Eckhart Tolle

As in so many other instances, the ultimate teaching of compassion came through my body. I had long dreamed of making a physical, architectural and spiritual pilgrimage out of the Inca Trail to the ancient ruins of Machu Picchu. The trail was listed as a challenging five-day trek at high altitudes, ranging from 11,000 to 14,000 feet above sea level. Since I was going alone, I saved for a while to take the trip with Wilderness Travel, reputed to be a premium adventure travel company in the United States.

Never before having done anything quite so physically challenging, and knowing that I had to overcome my damaged knees, I trained for an entire year, starting with longer walks in Seattle's many lush parks, and eventually expanding to more strenuous hikes in the beautiful North Cascades, with Jason. Often, the harder hikes would well up the pain and weakness in my knees, and along with physical pain would come more emotional pain from 'body memory.' Although I treated myself with compassion, I often found myself wishing that this wasn't the case, wishing my knees hadn't been hurt in violence.

Finally, in December of 2007, I flew into Cusco, an excited knot in my belly from anticipation of this incredible undertaking, joining a travel group comprised of folks who had come in pairs from all over the United States. I was its thirteenth and youngest member.

At first I did pretty well. Our trek leader, a hearty German named Peter, reinforced the importance of each of us hiking at our own pace, which was defined as one in which one could carry on a normal conversation without much difficulty breathing. In keeping my pace, I often found myself trailing the pack, and I struggled quite a bit with this. How could sixty- and even seventy-somethings hike faster than me? Why couldn't I do better? Self-compassion became difficult, but I stuck to my pace nevertheless.

After acclimating with an easier, rambling hike through the Urubamba valley, we entered progressively harder territory, with steep and hard granite steps, sometimes about eighteen inches in height. Though I got slower and more weak-kneed by the day, I continued on tenaciously. I found myself looking forward to upward climbs, because my heart proved stronger than my knees; each step downwards caused such excruciating pain in them.

Then came one of the most physically challenging days of my life: the third day of the trek, over Dead Woman's Pass. We had spent the first half of the day hiking through a beautiful rainforest, and I had caught enough of a chill to nearly become hypothermic. After thawing out at our lunch camp, I summoned fresh courage to get over the pass, but my body began to give up. Each step felt like a hard slam through my legs, sending shock waves into my knees and the rest of my body. I couldn't really stop to rest because I had fallen way behind the group, and the light was quickly falling. Normally, one of the local guides who shepherded the group would bring up the rear, but on this late afternoon, even he was nowhere to be seen.

In one particular stretch of steep, slippery downward steps, my legs began shaking so hard in stress that I couldn't be sure of them anymore. At one point, my knees gave in and I slipped, nearly falling down the hard and icy granite mountain. My shock at this possibility was extreme; I could fall to my death in this jagged stretch.

I trudged on, inching my way down at an excruciating, snail's pace, tears streaming down my face in agony. Finally he appeared, the young local who normally brought up the rear. He had come back in search of me because the entire group had already made it to base camp! From there on, he helped me by hand all the way down to camp, even carrying my little backpack. It took us another full hour to get there, and by the time we were walking into the campsite I could barely contain the deluge of tears.

Afterwards I lay in my tent, still shaking, icing my feet and knees, the last tears of pain already exhausted. I had done it, somehow, the hardest part of the five-day trek. But more importantly, I had done something else. Along with releasing my last tears of pain on those treacherous slopes of Dead Woman's Pass, I had also left behind the last of my anger, shame and regret at my injured knees.

All of a sudden, there were no more tears to cry and there was nothing more to forgive. I could have felt defeated; instead, I felt a quiet, peaceful acceptance. *I had fully accepted my body just as it was.* It was New Year's Eve, so I got up to celebrate with the rest of the group in our festively decorated dinner tent. And the next morning, on January 1 2008, a brand new person and body resumed the climb up to our next camp!

This experience taught me something incredible: In the deeper, calmer waters of the sea of compassion, there is no need for forgiveness to begin with. This is because one is simply in acceptance: One offers no resistance to what is. So, *there is nothing to forgive*! By accepting my body as-is, I had opened the doors to ultimate peace. And by accepting its limitations without any need for story or explanation rooted in the past, I had laid the foundation for an amazing change: My knees began to heal at a rapid pace, and I was subsequently able to take on greater amounts of physical activity without much pain!

Sometime in 2010, when Andrew and I had reconnected, we were talking about the challenges of entrepreneurship in the perilous times of economic recession. We were discussing his deep frustration with the way things were. Then I said it. "I've discovered that – paradoxically – one can only change something by first accepting it. Tangible, external change is brought about by changing oneself internally, through acceptance. As soon as I accept the way things are, the foundation for change is immediately laid."

He looked confused, and protested: "But that doesn't make any sense! How can I accept the way things are? Isn't that tantamount to agreeing with the status quo, to permitting mediocrity, to giving in? Isn't acceptance essentially the equivalent of defeat? How can anything change by accepting defeat? Explain to me what you mean by acceptance!" Just like I had done before, he too was confusing acceptance with concepts of right and wrong, or with resignation.

I became tongue-tied. Any verbal explanation would risk sounding like yet another New Age cliché. How could I explain my discovery, something I could so clearly know and experience, but not really articulate without reducing it to intellectual rhetoric?

So, perhaps the best way to understand acceptance is not by working too hard to define it, but by exploring how it *feels*. In my experience, whenever I have stepped into acceptance, I have also experienced feelings of grace, generosity, compassion, love, peace, harmony, lightness, and humor. Acceptance allows me to stop reacting and start *creating*. It opens possibility.

The opposite of acceptance is resistance. Resistance is accompanied by feelings of righteousness, anger, fear, disturbance, antagonism, disgruntlement, heaviness and sadness. Resistance and non-forgiveness are spiritual toxins that build up over time, leading to disease, and preventing the healing of our bodies, and the evolution of our souls. They hinder and stunt our inherent, immense and limitless creative capacity to effect and generate anything positive in the world.

I offer here, yet another bodily example. When I first started to get off all medication for my migraines, I had an opportunity to observe the huge rush of fear and struggle in me whenever a migraine attack began. My mind and body braced for the worst, preparing for what felt like an eternal, unbearable pain-episode.

Then one day, I realized that there was a choice to do just the opposite. Instead of resisting and rejecting the pain as something 'bad,' I could choose to accept it, even welcome it! So, I began moving *towards* the pain rather than against it, or running away from it. I attended to it without judgment, with gentleness, and with neutrality.[19]

As I began doing this, the pain was allowed to course through my body, rather than be lodged within it. Imagine that something fluid in nature wants to flow through me, and I resist it with an internal force, causing a dam-like structure to be erected. What is going to

---

19. I was able to do this with the observation technique I learned in Vipassana meditation.

happen to the energy of the fluid against the dam? It is going to surge, swell and lash against the resistance. But if I remove the resistance, it is going to flow through me. What came into me from the Universe must flow back into the Universe; it is the natural law of Physics! I began noticing that every time I was able to accept the pain and experience it as a strong river flowing through me, its course was expedited. I received relief sooner and sooner over time.[20]

Acceptance is not concerned with what or who is right, or with concepts of good and bad. Neither is it a state of passive resignation. It is achieved by stepping aside from being right, to actively and lovingly observing *what is*. Acceptance, therefore, is the non-judgmental witnessing of (and not necessarily agreement or compliance with) whatever is. Such witnessing allows the negative feelings of resistance to surface, be observed, and then also be accepted. So, acceptance is the cessation of resistance. And when resistance ceases internally, then resistance ceases externally too, and the doors for change are opened.

From Acceptance to Pure Love:
Love is Not Fear

"There are four elements of true love.... The third element of true love is joy, or mudita. If there is no joy in love, it is not true love. The fourth element of true love is upeksha, equanimity or freedom. In true love, you attain freedom. When you love, you bring freedom to the person you love…not only outside but also inside."

– Thich Nhat Hanh

A$t the root of compassion, of course, is love: pure and unfettered. But what *is* love?

---

20. Over more time I recognized, of course, that resistance – of all forms – was the root cause of my migraines in the first place! By continuing this practice, I was able to minimize and alleviate my migraines naturally, each and every time. Eventually I used this approach for all other physical ailments!

When I first experienced seeing my purer nature in the mirror that is Andrew — when my highest potential was revealed and summoned — I didn't remotely know what to call the immense force that throbbed inside my chest, breaking it open and threatening to gush forth into the world. 'Love' is the only word I had in my vocabulary.

It is only with my deepening spiritual awakening that the nature of pure love began to reveal itself to me. Although what I had felt initially with Andrew had some dependence, need and fear of loss associated with it, with my deepening awakening, it transmuted from a feeling into a powerful, free, joyful and *active* force. This force does gush into the world, but it does so as a vibrant, creative energy. It is loving not only towards him, but towards all beings, always including my own self. It is secure, still, peaceful, and all-knowing. While it continues to be tender and vulnerable, this love is not saddled with need, obligation, expectation, fear, pain, lack, or loss. It knows, without a doubt, its power, vitality and immortality. And it sees that its divine purpose extends beyond the drama of physical and emotional existence; it has *soul work* to do! It is a guiding compass and a generative force, creating every moment of my thriving life and all its labors of love. It *is* my Higher Power!

Like many of us, I too grew up with a particular construct of love, including romantic love. In my family narrative, love was the passionate force that compelled my young parents to elope at the mere ages of nineteen and twenty-one, fleeing from their parents who were using the Hindu caste system as a weapon of destruction. Yet, it was that same love that gave rise to expectations and disappointments, and quickly, disintegrated and destroyed their marriage and the safety and innocence of my childhood. From all accounts, love was also the intense feeling my mother experienced when she had me, and yet, that same love was what drove her to be possessive and even divisive, to gain my complete, unquestioning loyalty towards her and her suffering. Love drove my father astray from his marriage, but then, love also brought him back to his family.

On television, Bollywood movies implied that love conquered all evil, and that love transcended differences of religion, caste and class. Yet, that same love was the source of jealousy, warring families, separation, worry, guilt, pain, anguish, and even death!

Fueled by what I had learned from these familial, social and cultural cues, as well as the first teenage crushes resulting from my changing biology, I too began to experience romantic love as a strange concoction of attraction and anguish, of expectation and disappointment. It was defined by mystery and uncertainty, underlying which was, really, a fear of rejection and loss. Through all these experiences and conditionings, love also came to be associated with pain.

Yet, when I remember back to an age as early as eight or nine, I had a clear and un-ambiguous sense of love that had nothing whatsoever to do with fear or pain. It was in my intrinsic nature to know how to open my heart and express my caring: freely and fearlessly. What had changed over time? Why hadn't this way of loving stayed intact? Why had this pure, essential way of loving been marred and obscured by pain and fear, guilt and shame?

When my love for Andrew compelled me to find my own center, to connect with my Higher Power and eventually, to connect with the compassion of the Universe, I was able to remember and access again, the early, pure and untainted love with which I had originally entered this world. Rapidly, my false constructs of love began to disintegrate. Following this, those relationships of mine that were based on such constructs also began to either disintegrate or transform. Pure, essential love began to distinguish itself from the constructs of love that are prevalent all around us: romantic, parental, friendship-based or otherwise. These, I realized, are nothing but love's opposite force – fear – in action.

Consider this common parental or romantic refrain, (one which I too have igno-rantly employed many a time), "I worry about you because I love you." If one is brutally honest, this sentiment is driven by fear, not love. It has little to do with the loved one's well-being, and is centered entirely on one's own fears of loss or pain. Proclamations such as, "I love you so much, I wish you'd never leave my side," "I feel jealous because I love you," and "I love you so much I cannot live without you," are other examples of fear-based mental states, not love-based consciousness.

Fear also underlies other manipulative devices commonly deployed in the name of love: guilt, shame, disapproval. "If you loved me you'd do this for me," uses fear in the form of threat or conditionality. Even positive, approval- and praise-laden statements, such as, "You've been so good, I love you," are based in conditionality, instilling a subliminal fear that this love can just as easily be withdrawn should the receiver cease to be 'good' in the way that the love-giver defines, desires or demands.

Since budding romantic love is kindled by mystery and uncertainty – that is, a fear of loss – it follows that it, in itself, is *not* pure love. Given my romantic attachment with the concept of romance, this was a rather unsettling, if not devastating insight to have gained. For months I struggled with it and its implications: I didn't want to give up the thrill, the excitement, the tummy-tingling typically associated with romantic love!

My understanding expanded and deepened when I read *The Road Less Traveled*, the classic work of M. Scott Peck. In this profound book that has impacted millions, Peck sheds loving light on the nature of love itself: "*Love is not a feeling; it is an action*," he says. 'Falling in love' is a chemical and physiological process that is both temporary and illusory, designed to get us to bond and procreate.

Yet, 'falling in love' is also the spark – the opening – that has the potential to start a journey of conscious, meaningful, purposeful loving, Peck observes through his many years of counseling experience and spiritual revelations. In other words, falling in love is the opening of possibility, for the experience and practice of pure love. Sexual love is the doorway to the path of spiritual love. It is a uniquely human opportunity to recognize this incredible potential of sexual and romantic love, and to harness it.

So, what does "love is an action" really mean? Does it mean that love is duty or obligation? Does it mean sticking with someone through thick and thin, no matter what? Not really. As I began to check my fear-based actions in various relationships, I began to see that love as an action means that it is, first and foremost, a choice. It is conscious and purposeful. It is a constant, disciplined practice. It is compassionate, forgiving, and accepting. It rises beyond conditionality, judgment, and constructs of right and wrong. Love is effortful; love is hard. Yet, because pure love is the opposite of fear, *it is also not pain*. It is not anguish, guilt, shame, embarrassment, obligation, anxiety or worry. And it is certainly not driven by need, desperation or dependence.

I like to say that pure love is *effortful, purposeful, joyful, creative* and *liberating* action. If it is not joyful, if it comes at personal harm or toxicity, then it is not love but co-dependence, another fear-driven condition. In situations of toxicity or co-dependence, "love is an action" actually translates to letting the person go (with love)! If it isn't liberating – setting oneself and one's beloved free – then it isn't love. Finally, if it isn't productive and generative in joyful and positive ways in the world, then too it isn't love!

These days, I know I am being truly loving when I am being courageous, when I have no personal motivation or agenda, when it is hard work, and when it causes me *and* my loved one to spiritually grow and transform in meaningful ways, while never diminishing my or my loved one's essential spirit. Pure love is never a zero sum game: It is abundant, and everyone gains and wins.

Knowing and practicing pure love is absolutely fundamental to a thriving life. Love creates, and creativity spurs a thriving life. Love *is* Creation, and Creation *is* love. Love is *dharma*; love is *karma*; love is *moksha*. Love is everything.

In forgiveness is my freedom

Compassion is my connection with the loving, benevolent, and forgiving force of the Universe, resulting in the cultivation of the same within me, activating true healing and authentic power.

Compassion in action is:

– Trusting completely in the immense benevolent, forgiving, loving force in the Universe, letting go of all personal control of ourcomes;

– Radiating freely towards oneself and others, an active, loving energetic state of being, like the sun's radiant, warm, healing and empowering energy;

– Seeing that clinging to rightness energizes the very negative force one is 'fighting,' and knowing that detachment from rightness does not mean condoning or perpetuating injustice; therefore directing all energy to loving inner change as a way to transform the world;

– Realizing that in the deeper, calmer waters of one's core, there is no need for forgiveness to begin with, because one is simply in acceptance, without resistance to *what is*;

– Finding, ultimately, in one's center, pure and unfettered love: love that is an effortful, purposeful, joyful, creative and liberating action, the antithesis of fear.

Like centering and consciousness, compassion also requires daily practice. Whenever I become unduly upset about a situation, it is a sign that I am being unforgiving and non-compassionate, at the root of which is always fear. As soon as I replace fear with love, I am reconnected with the radiant state of being and I am empowered to take transformative, creative action. Compassion becomes a natural way of being when I stay connected to the pure love in my core, the very foundation for a thriving, creative life.

For Jason

4.
CHOICE

Choice is the ability to freely and unequivocally select a path revealed lovingly and organically when I submit to my Higher Power, beyond and independent of the mental processes of reason, rationality, obligation, and constructs of 'right' and 'wrong.'

I always have a choice

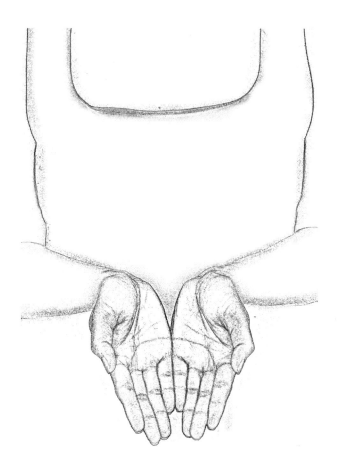

Decision Or Choice:
Because I Just Do!

"Life is a sum of all your choices."

– Albert Camus

Even as an insatiable language enthusiast who revels in the nuances of words, for most of my life, I had used the words choice and decision interchangeably. "Come on, hurry up and decide!" or, "Come on, hurry up and choose!" sound quite the same to most ears and minds, don't they?

In the summer of 2005, at the urging of my colleague and friend Paula, I had enrolled myself in the Landmark Forum.[21] Countless transformative insights revealed themselves to me in that intense three-day weekend of unraveling the concepts of past and related self-constructs, but one of my biggest takeaways was an awareness of the significant difference between a decision and a choice. While this distinction struck an immediate chord with me that weekend, it has taken several years of iterations, and a deepening consciousness to translate it into consistent action.

A wildly energetic, forceful, and convincing ex-military man named Jan was conducting the Forum. Over the course of the three intense days Jan ran several interactive exercises, in each of which a handful of the hundred participants usually became his mediums to extract and illustrate key insights. In one exercise, he put two women and a man in the hot seats center-stage, and asked them a seemingly trivial question: "Which between chocolate and vanilla flavors of ice-cream is your favorite?" As soon as the person picked a flavor, he pressed, "Why?"

This follow-up question usually resulted in puzzled looks, followed by responses that explained the individual's reasons for the preference. One person might have said, "Well, chocolate, because its flavors are deeper and richer...," while another might have offered, "Vanilla because it is mild and always goes with everything..." Jan would promptly

---

21. The Landmark Forum is a program offered by Landmark Education LLC, a prominent personal training and development company founded in 1991, which offers educational programs worldwide.

and aggressively cut them short and practically yell, "Tell me again, *why?*" Now the poor scapegoats looked frightened, and went into further stammering elaborations to defend their preference, floundering for the right answer that would please the whip-cracking master. No answer seemed good enough, and Jan kept pressing them, demanding incessantly, why, why, why? Then suddenly, one of the women's faces cracked open in tearful exasperation. She stamped her foot, and yelled back indignantly, "*Because*! I *just* like it!"

In an instant, Jan's face relaxed into a calm and kindly demeanor, and I felt the steamy pressure in the room release like a pressure-cooker cooling.[22] The young woman who had just exploded was now pretty much crying, and Jan walked up to her and placed his hand reassuringly on her shoulder. "Congratulations," he said softly, "You have just made a choice." She looked baffled, quite oblivious to why yelling back at him had produced such an unexpected result of warmth and approval. Jan then turned to the whiteboard and wrote out the following:

– DECISION: A path selected as an outcome of various rational considerations.

– CHOICE: A path selected after all rational considerations have been made, examined, and set aside.

In other words, reasoning out a path through rational considerations leads to a decision, whereas, conducting the reasoning and then putting it aside (or sometimes, skipping it altogether) to move towards what *feels* right is a choice. When I talk of feeling, however, I don't mean a slew of random emotions. That would only result in more decisions, only emotional decisions instead of rational ones! I mean the intuitive sense of "this is right for me" that arises out of stillness. And such feeling is, paradoxically, characterized by a state of detachment and neutrality towards the available options. It is free of any urgency or compulsion to go one way or another. It's the peaceful feeling that arises out of the position: "Well, I could go this way, or I could go that way, and either way would be quite fine…but, I freely and intentionally choose this, *just because it feels right.*"

There are other ways in which I have learned to distinguish between the two. A decision can be explained, a choice simply exists. A decision comes from the mind; a choice comes from the gut (or the heart). A decision is based on rationalizations; a choice is based

---

22. Through the course of the weekend I grew to admire Jan's well-practiced ability and loving intention in putting on the pressure when necessary, and recognized that it was always done with expert and conscious control.

on faith. A decision is often obligatory to others; a choice is not burdensome (even if it is made in order to help others). A decision might be second-guessed; a choice is rarely prone to doubt. A decision is laborious; a choice is fun. A decision leaves us with a feeling of compromise; a choice gives us contentment. Above all, you know you are exercising choice when you are *free* to embrace your path, even if it is the *only* option you have!

Why work so hard to make this seemingly semantic distinction? I've found that the difference between decision and choice is terribly significant because it is the difference between surviving and thriving. Our society has become riddled and crippled with decision-making, and we have forgotten to make a real choice, simple and straight. We have forgotten to be comfortable and confident about what our internal compass – our Higher Power – tells us. Instead, we second-guess our internal guide and we ask others for advice, conduct Google searches, make spreadsheets with weighted factors, and *calculate* our way forward.

For those of us who have endured toxic situations, whether personal or professional, distinguishing between decision and choice can become even more difficult. This is because, quite ironically, the more hostile the environment, the greater the rationalization one undertakes to explain away the reasons for the toxicity, and the reasons for maintaining the status quo. And most often this rationalization keeps one hostage in a harmful, unhealthy environment that in turn, further chips away and erodes one's recognition of choice, perpetuating the cycle of toxicity. One fails to see that when one listens intently to one's internal compass, it always reveals the right path, promptly and unequivocally.

The causes for not making choices are many. Society, our typical upbringing in terms of constructs of 'right' and 'wrong,' and the accumulation of knowledge together conspire to condition us to be 'rational' and 'reasonable,' or, "do the right thing." Do you think a child ever makes decisions? Aadit, my friend and business partner Shirin's five-year-old son, is always perplexed when asked why he wants what he wants. "Because I just do!" he exclaims, without missing a heartbeat.

As we grow into adults, caution and risk-management strap us in, and we become people who *manage* resources and outcomes, forgetting to *lead* our lives. We discern fewer and fewer opportunities to make choices. We no longer give ourselves permission to be unreasonable, afraid that if we haven't mapped out all options and considerations and weighed them carefully to select a path, we will be wrong, and we will miserably fail. Fear of failure, or of losing something else in return for making a straightforward choice cripples us, and often the only types of choice we allow ourselves as adults are, perhaps, limited to the flavor of ice-cream or the clothing we want to wear on a given day. (Sometimes those things too become riddled with external considerations!)

One of the major events in the last seven years, in which I had the opportunity to practice choice, was my starting to date in mid-2006, for the first time since my marriage ended. Or I should probably say, for the first time ever, since I married so young and all my 'boyfriends' prior were circumstantial, while the 'dating' my ex-husband and I had done was limited to letters across international borders and a handful of outings when we visited each other in India or America during our brief courtship. Needless to say, dating for the first time at the age of thirty-two after a spiritual awakening was a singular experience!

I observed my mind playing its usual rational games while evaluating suitors: this person has a graduate degree and that person doesn't; this person works in a responsible position and that person needs some growing up...and so on. But, perhaps for the first time in my life, I was also conscious and respectful of my instincts, and allowed them to navigate the more so-called primitive aspects like chemistry and attraction, which are essentially 'unreasonable.'

In the end, I found myself making choices beyond the mind: free of the burden of reason. This is not to be mistaken for emotional or erratic caprice; rather, it was the ability to connect with my Higher Power and allow it to guide me. I discovered that my choices had little correlation with what I thought of a particular person in terms of *his* specific attributes and qualities, and instead, had much more to do with how I felt about *myself* when with that person! If I liked and enjoyed myself, I stuck with it!

But wait, while this was straightforward, it doesn't mean it was easy! It is terribly difficult to always like yourself in a relationship. It requires deep self-awareness, consciousness and compassion. It behooves one to constantly observe one's motivations in the mirror of the relationship, and lovingly course-correct when the image staring back isn't so pretty, not in a self-sacrificing way but in an effortful, 'love-as-an-action' kind of way. One simply doesn't get to make a project out of the other person, but must turn the focus inward at every turn! In short, it requires unconditional love.

This is how an otherwise highly unlikely partnership formed between Jason and I for over three years, and it is also how we knew when to dissolve the romantic relationship. And finally, it is how we transitioned into a mutually supportive friendship. I can fairly say that my unconditional love for Andrew matured into a continued practice through my significant relationship with Jason. All this, because I connected with choice!

I have come to recognize that in a life of thriving, the more often we make choices the greater our contentment, and through our choices, greater the welfare of others in our lives as well. Choice liberates us from the artificial pressures of circumstance, and it makes each one of us responsible for leading our own paths. Each of us was born with a powerful internal compass, lovingly and freely gifted to us. A life of choice-making led by one's internal compass is a life of thriving. I tell myself often: Go ahead, be *un*reasonable!

Reaction, Response, Or Initiation:
Take Initiative!

"From a peaceful center we can respond instead of react. Unconscious reactions create problems. Considered responses bring peace."

– Jack Kornfield

Although dating was – no pun intended – a hotbed of insight, it was while working in the fast-paced, aggressive corporate environment that I had an experience fully illustrating how recognizing and exercising choice immensely benefits actions and outcomes.

In the summer of 2007, I was instrumental in helping the global design firm I worked in, win a project with a powerful organization in Asia, with a long historic, institutional and prestigious legacy. This client sought to revitalize their product offerings, and rejuvenate their entire client base. And I was to develop and facilitate a process of engagement and customer discovery, which our team could then translate into a design vision for a new masterplan.

The project was housed in the Los Angeles office of the firm, and working with the people there ended up being one of the most transformative and delightful experiences of my entire eight-year career with the firm. The young leaders of the L.A. office were visionary, talented, secure and collaborative in the truest sense, transcending the political maneuvering, big-firm inertia and status-quo clinging I had often encountered in other parts of the firm. One of the leaders, Robert, was the project manager for this new demanding Asia project, and we spent enough time together to also become good friends and true partners in project leadership. (From winning the project in May, through November that year, I traveled to Asia five times, and I practically lived in Los Angeles at other times!)

Now, although the client's stated vision read as an extraordinary endeavor when we started out with the project, we soon began to encounter some tough hurdles that were also the obvious reasons for their not having achieved their vision thus far. The closer we got to understanding them, the more we saw that while certain members of their executive leadership had set their sights high, those in charge of managing these laudable goals were so unbelievably fear-driven, that all their actions were merely reactionary to the daily tide of events within the organization. (To be fair, this particular phenomenon is in some degree or another, typical for any large organization anywhere in the world.) The events impacting project decisions in this case, however, were driven by power, prestige and politics laced with a peculiar blend of traditional Asian culture and lingering colonial flavors within the organization, the mysterious workings of which we failed to fully comprehend.

On top of all this, we had a project manager on the client-side – let's call him Mr. Hui – who turned out to be one of the biggest control freaks I have ever encountered. While he was undoubtedly knowledgeable and was, rightly, our primary source of information, he crossed the line by fancying himself as a designer in disguise, and by presenting himself as the ultimate authority on all aspects of the design problem (including every concern related to customers, product offerings or the business workings in general) in a way that we – ostensibly the talented team of strategic design thinkers – were essentially rendered useless.

In fact, quickly, it began to appear that Mr. Hui had just wanted (expensive) hired help to draw per his bidding and scheming, rather than leverage their talents to collaborate with him and his team in any significant, strategic, or meaningful way. He had us chasing our tails like mad little slave animals, demanding that we show up in Asia and practically live under his nose. (He would arrive unannounced at our hotel lobby and ring our rooms!) During the intervals in which we were back home in North America, he wanted to hear from us several times a day. He kept constant tabs on us; he called incessantly on our mobile phones, including at odd hours of the night, and generated a nonstop stream of mindless tasks that had nothing whatsoever to do with the critical workflow on the project.

In return he expected impressive quantities of faxes and emails, adding up to a paper trail that we were working fulltime just to generate, successfully clogging up the virtual world's channels with nothing but gibberish. Eventually, he also began to threaten that he would show up at our U.S. offices at short notice, and this usually succeeded in sending us into fresh, frenetic rounds of frantically paced busywork just to please the insatiable Mr. Hui, and prevent him from unexpectedly setting foot anywhere near the west coast of America.

Soon, Robert's and my fulltime jobs entailed keeping Mr. Hui temporarily fed and at bay, so that other team members were free to do the actual work. Quickly, however, we found that like a virulent virus, Mr. Hui had eaten through our valiantly constructed fort walls; his demands and machinations required yet another living brain and yet another living brain and yet another…to be sacrificed to the guillotine of 'client satisfaction.' Pretty soon, not one team member was left to do any truly creative work towards the heroic and monumental task of revitalizing a withering civic venue and legacy! No, we had all turned into Mr. Hui's obedient house-servants and drycleaners.

One day Robert and I had had enough. We knew that this situation was untenable; we were exhausted and depleted, directionless and uncreative as a team. Talking it over, we wondered what would happen if we simply slowed things down, and allowed some lapses between Mr. Hui's various requests and demands that came through each day, and our responses to them. Better still, we wondered what would happen if we simply didn't respond at all to about half of them. (Much of this conversation on the phone was occurring through a delirious mass of giggles late in the evening, a side-effect of our exhausted state, but we were quite serious about this strategy.) From the next day we put this into practice, and began ignoring Mr. Hui's stream of messages, while directing the team to do work based on our own assessment and creative initiative about what needed to be done next.

An amazing thing happened: Mr. Hui began outdating himself daily! Say he sent us an assignment on a Monday, based on some internal organizational directive that he imagined to be terribly relevant to the project, then by Tuesday, he might change his mind saying, "Don't bother doing that, but do this instead," based usually on however the wind had changed direction within his organization that morning. Then if we responded with a simple "Okay," and maintained our gall to ignore the new directive for a bit, we would often receive updated instructions by Thursday. By this time, we would have bought ourselves three or four days of clear time to work, and on late Thursday, we could take some time to respond as thoughtfully and meaningfully as possible to the latest version of the 'request.' In this manner, Robert and I reclaimed our team's sanity, perspective, initiative, and creative direction.[23]

Through this experience it became evident that when faced with difficult and noisy external circumstances – technically known as firefighting in corporatespeak – it is easy to become consumed and begin to autopilot under the illusion that we have limited or no choice. Most of us *react* to these stressful situations, a handful *respond*, while very, very few of us actually *initiate* meaningful action.[24] I find that when I am exercising choice, I am usually initiating action rather than reacting or responding to external circumstances.

Choice in Action:
The 48-hour Emergency Rule

"You do not need to leave your room. Remain sitting at your table and listen. Do not even listen, simply wait, be quiet, still and solitary. The world will freely offer itself to you to be unmasked, it has no choice, it will roll in ecstasy at your feet."

– Franz Kafka

After my discovery that initiating, as opposed to reacting or even responding, is the secret to exercising choice, I began wondering how I might replace (mental) reactivity with (spiritual) initiative in a sustained, habitual way. The first and most obvious thing seemed to be to introduce time: "Sleep over it!," as wise elders would've said. But introducing time alone can be passive, and not necessarily a cure to reactivity. This is because

---

23. It's relevant to mention that we did have to part ways with the client eventually, and did not take the masterplan project beyond early strategic schemes based on the customer discovery. While this was a great regret for the some of the firm's leadership, I never felt for a moment that it was the 'wrong' outcome for the firm. Had we forced ourselves to stay on that project, we would have squandered away precious resources in futility for several years!

24. This particular framework of thinking about choice crystallized for me much later, while reading a section in Seth Godin's wonderful book *Tribes*.

in the short term, affording space and time increases the reactivity of the mind, causing to surface greater and deeper fears that would have otherwise remained repressed, had I allowed myself to react immediately. So, I wondered, when introducing time what *active* stance could I take without *acting out*, to calm the noise, mitigate reactivity, and allow the right choice to emerge from my innate wisdom, from my Higher Power?

In the chapter Centering, I described how listening to my body – placing "matter over mind"– provided a guide for navigating situations. So, I already had an inkling that my body held the key to truths my mind didn't know, and therefore, significant clues for making choices. Then in 2008, I learned the meditative practice of Vipassana, which not only exponentially deepened my awareness of my body, but also provided me with an essential methodology for detached observation that allows innate wisdom to arise. Over days of keenly and non-judgmentally observing my breath and body sensations, I witnessed deeply held psychosomatic experiences arise, and then pass out of my system, leaving behind an emptiness from which real wisdom could initiate.

Based on Vipassana method, I invented a little rule, which I named *The 48-hour Emergency Rule*. It goes as follows. Whenever I experience a stressful, anxiety-ridden situation – an 'emergency' – in which I feel the urgency to take immediate action, I make myself pause and pose the question: *If I do nothing for twenty-four hours, will anyone's life be at risk?* If the answer is "No," which it is nearly hundred-percent of the time, I do nothing outwardly for twenty-four hours. "Doing nothing" means not only taking no outward action regarding the situation, but also not talking to anybody at all about it, not sending emails, not even making oblique references; nothing at all.

This do-nothing period, however, is not a passive, un-intentional one. Much to the contrary, while I do nothing outwardly, internally I undertake Vipassana: I heighten my awareness, and observe all my reactions, thoughts and feelings, including all my bodily sensations. I acknowledge and accept them, and I let them pass through me. (If I absolutely must 'do' something, I write my observations down in a private place.) Then when twenty-four hours are up, I ask myself the same question again: *If I do nothing for twenty-four hours, will anyone's life be at risk?* If the answer continues to be "No," I follow the same procedure for another twenty-four hours.

Practicing in this way, I found that typically, within forty-eight hours, one of four things happens with an amazing certainty:

– The right course of action reveals itself clearly and unequivocally, or
– New information or circumstances emerge, making further reflection necessary (and also rendering useless any action I might have initially taken), or
– Someone or something else takes care of the problem and it goes away, or
– The urgency of the problem disappears, and I feel no need to do anything at all!

Although I originally invented *The 48-hour Emergency Rule* for situations with a context of urgency, this was only the starting point for a rigorous practice of choice. As many leadership coaches tell us, we are wired to equate 'urgent' with 'important' – effecting a flight-or-fight response – so, it was easier to use the sense of urgency as a sign to pause and exercise choice. In truth, of course, this is a way of being that can be practiced at all times and in any context.

Typically, we react all the time in seemingly innocuous, everyday situations, forgetting that it is completely in our power (and terribly important) to pace ourselves and initiate the right action from a place of choice. The phone rings and one jumps habitually to answer it, even if one is eating a quiet, relaxed meal. A friend asks to go out on a Friday evening, and one thinks one must go, since one doesn't have formal plans for that evening anyway. A boss says the next project is going to be big and exciting, and one forgets to consider if big-and-exciting is what one necessarily wants all the time. A boyfriend offers to buy one a new dress for an upcoming birthday, and one doesn't stop to wonder if there's a need for one more piece of clothing hanging in the closet.

It might seem that it would be easy to recognize and exercise choice in these mundane and commonplace situations, but many of us rarely do. We don't even see that it is terribly important that we do, that it leads to the 'right' thing, not only for ourselves, but also for the others involved. We continue on reactively, saying yes or no, but not seeing that we could pause and listen patiently for a *third* way: the way of our spirit, the way of initiative. And then we wonder why we feel obligated, exhausted or blue most of the time!

So, once I had *The 48-hour Emergency Rule* relatively mastered in situations of 'urgency,' I also began to treat non-urgent situations as 'important,' and practiced pacing myself, remembering and exercising choice in these as well. I found myself feeling lighter, happier and more genuinely compassionate and kind to others!

The 48-hour Emergency Rule is exceedingly simple yet challenging to apply because of our ingrained habits, and the mind's tendency for reactivity. But when I persevere with it and practice it regularly, it never fails me! Every time and in every situation, it enables choice to emerge beyond the traps of mental analysis, ruminations and rationalizations, and makes for the right path.

Toppling Co-dependence: *Where's the Velcro?*

"I am the captain of my soul."

– Nelson Mandela

Recognizing and exercising choice is hardest when unwittingly or otherwise, we become co-dependent in situations or relationships. Co-dependence, as I've written about at some length in the chapter Compassion, is the tendency to behave in overly caretaking ways that often involves putting one's needs at a lower priority than those of others. While healthy kindness, compassion and helpfulness towards others do not come at severe costs to oneself, co-dependence is characterized by 'the need to be needed,' and can result in either self-deprecating behaviors on one extreme, or controlling behaviors on the other, thus damaging one's life, health and relationships.

When one has been in toxic romantic, family, work or societal situations for long durations, co-dependence can become a survival mechanism, because caretaking, heroism and other behaviors that feed the needs of the aggressor or narcissist or dominant as may be the case, appear to be the safest thing to do for short-term self-preservation. But eventually, playing either the victim or the hero can become a convenient habit, both because it is comfortable, and because it becomes a way to avoid personal responsibility. I've observed that people can become co-dependent even in socio-political phenomena such as racism, sexism, classism or political oppression. In these situations, the very people with the complaint often subconsciously maintain the victim or hero status, because there is a latent psychological payoff in the form of affirmation, approval, recognition, and validation.

Before one knows it, the habitual victim or hero status can lead one to entirely forget that there is choice at every turn: even when one is in an abusive relationship, even when one is in the minority population in a racist society, even when one is oppressed in a political dictatorship, and so on. This choice isn't about morality in the absolute sense; it's about knowing one's worth in one's own heart in no uncertain terms. So, there is *always* a choice; at the very least, there is a choice to see the situation differently in one's heart – uniquely and creatively – and this shift in perspective becomes the first seed of change. As soon as one remembers choice, one takes back authentic power. Initiative is taken, not given!

So, the most complex aspect of recognizing and exercising choice, especially in 'negative' situations, is parsing apart possible options even if there appear to be none. It always helps me to ask myself some difficult questions: How am I participating in perpetuating negativity? What is my contribution, if any: Am I playing the victim or hero role here? Is there a latent payoff for me that keeps me in this situation, or maintains the status-quo, or makes me see the situation in a disempowering way? How can I take responsibility? How can I take initiative, and make a choice? How can I take back my power, and to do so, what uncomfortable changes would I have to make, or which payoffs would I have to relinquish?

My shorthand for undertaking such a self-inquiry is: "Where is the Velcro?" The property of Velcro is that it adheres with a vengeance, but only when the corresponding piece is available to stick with. So, I began imagining that in every situation giving rise to negative feelings and responses in me such as hurt, offense, or oppression, there had to be a corresponding piece of Velcro hiding somewhere inside me, for the negative feeling to stick with. Otherwise, I was convinced, it simply wouldn't stick. It wouldn't be personal; it wouldn't be about me. And so, it wouldn't have any power over me either. I would be free; I would have a choice; I would have authentic power.

A telling example that leaps to mind is a challenging situation I experienced in my relationship with Jason. About a year-and-a-half into our dating, upon meeting me for the first (and only) time, Jason's mother launched an exhaustive campaign against me, simply because I am not Christian. Writing lengthy and elaborate email manifestos to her son, she spent an extraordinary amount of energy in this effort, doing everything from making speculations and insinuations about Indians and Hindus, to downright character assassination of me based on my life trajectory, including my divorce, my eventual leap off a corporate career, or even my ongoing participation in Seattle's *Yoni ki Baat*.[25] At first I was baffled, then deeply hurt. And finally I was enraged, especially when I experienced Jason blow off as "mom just being mom," what I perceived as bigoted and racist attacks against me. I thought then that he was minimizing my hurt and the gravity of the situation.[26]

I spent hours in turmoil over Jason's mother's words about me, finding loopholes in her arguments, and found myself so deeply disturbed that I became obsessed with the nitty-gritty of the teachings of Christianity. Having had a rather special place in my heart for Jesus and his example since I was a little girl, I was desperate to understand if there is any institutionalized prejudice against people of other faiths in Christianity's core teachings. What's more, I also found myself suddenly feeling defensive about Hinduism, even though I had never considered myself a practicing Hindu, or for that matter, a practitioner of any organized religion at all. My spirituality was entirely my own, something that had awakened organically in my thirties, through my own insights and revelations; yet, all of a sudden, I felt uncharacteristically and passionately protective of my cultural and religious heritage.

The more I searched for answers, obsessing over the various religious teachings and belief systems, the less I got anywhere at all. And meanwhile, my relationship with Jason suffered serious blows, and his mother's vicious attacks continued unabated. I began having a deeply negative experience, suffering constant distress and agony. The more I felt this way, the more I sought opportunities to prove Jason wrong about his ways around this conflict, or prove his mother wrong in her actions, when neither of these needed any proving at all. Soon, I rather resembled her, collecting tomes from my own research, and writing up long manifestos about why *I* was right. I had become the defiant victim!

And then suddenly, I saw it: the matching Velcro inside me. Even though Jason's mother's actions may have been hurtful or even morally wrong, there was the corresponding piece of Velcro inside me that was hooking her behavior. Some bizarre insecurity lurked inside me, which either unconsciously sought her approval, or desperately needed her to respect my culture and heritage, the identity of which I was mistakenly equating to the essence of me. What's more, I was evidently also insecure in my relationship with Jason, equating his passive way of relating with conflict (both with his mother and with me), to a lack of caring for me.

---

25. A powerful and transformative staged show created from a growing repository of original stories of womanhood and sexuality by local South Asian women, inspired by Eve Ensler's Vagina Monologues.

26. I eventually came to understand that Jason believed that giving his mother's actions any attention at all was the equivalent of energizing the issue.

What I could have chosen to view as sheer ignorance in Jason's mother or undeveloped conflict-resolution skills in Jason, I had turned instead, into an ongoing, deeply negative cycle in which I too had become an active participant. I was either the victim of Jason's mother's actions, or the hero in 'solving' the conflict resolution issues I had with Jason. In playing either role, I took away the possibility for the others to change behavior or take responsibility. I had forgotten that I had a choice to take a different path altogether!

Once I realized what I was doing, I recalled the insights I've shared in the chapter Compassion: that I had a choice to unhook from the drama and negativity, that I had a choice "to be right or to be happy," *that I had a choice at all.* I stopped focusing on Jason's mother and her actions, and I stopped wondering and obsessing about the various religious frameworks I had been researching. Instead, I recognized the terrible fear at the root of his mother's actions, and I simply returned to what I had come to know best in my own organically evolving spiritual path – compassion and forgiveness – leading immediately to peace within myself.

Miraculously, in a short period of time, Jason's mother's emails stopped flooding his inbox. No, she didn't fall in love with me, but the venom stopped flowing my way. Jason and I had an opportunity to at least begin our own dialogue, without his mother and her opinions looming over us like an ominous shadow.

"Where's the Velcro?" has become a powerful metaphor for me, to help me always return to choice, no matter how dismal or challenging the external circumstances might appear. Over time I have become practiced in recognizing how I am hooking the circumstances, and how I can make the choice to unhook. Situations that appear impossible – whether at work, in social situations, in creative collaborations, or in personal relationships – begin to rapidly become de-energized, disempowered or diffused as soon as I unhook, as soon as I dissolve the corresponding piece of Velcro inside me. Always and without fail, making a simple internal choice changes external circumstances for me. Once again, Gandhi's incredible guidance, *Be the change you wish to see in the world,* acquired new and deeper levels of meaning!

The Ultimate Choice:
Choosing What I Have

"Success is getting what you want. Happiness is wanting what you get."

– Dave Gardner

So far I've been discussing choice in contexts in which there exists the possibility of multiple options. But what about a situation in which there truly appears to be only one possible path to take? Does that leave one with choice?

As I exercised choice in various life situations, I stumbled upon the strangest and most paradoxical of truths: the ultimate exercise in choice, in such a single-option situation, *is to choose what I have*, whether I 'like' the option or not! Wait, that sounds ridiculous, you say! What does it mean to choose what one already has? Where's the choice in the matter? And isn't that counter-intuitive and contrary to all the insights offered thus far in this chapter, most of all, that "I always have a choice"? Well, no, it's not, because *I always have the choice to choose what I have!*

We tend to assume that when we are in a situation that we would like to change because it is unpleasant or doesn't meet our needs or values, exercising choice automatically implies either resisting or moving away from what we already have. But there are many situations (including multiple-option ones!), in which choice might imply consciously leaning *into* the situation: choosing it, embracing it, accepting it, truly and purely loving it. Now, why is this important? Why should I choose what I have? The answer lies in the insight on acceptance that I shared in the chapter Compassion: how, paradoxically, acceptance is a powerful way to allow any situation to transmute or transform itself. Choosing what I have is a defining moment in that process. Not choosing what I have builds resistance, and therefore, inner and outer toxicity.

The meaning of 'choosing what I have' is that I no longer simply linger or drag in a negative situation because "I don't have a choice," but I actively, consciously, authentically and lovingly choose the existing situation as mine. Lingering in a situation and choosing a situation are vastly different, even though in appearance, they might look like identical courses of action. The energetic quality behind each is different: One is passive, the other is active; one is denial, the other is conscious; one is fearful, the other is loving.

For me, 'choosing what I have' became clear through the healing of my relationship with my parents. I had successfully forgiven, moved past hurts, and accepted my turbulent childhood as it had been. And in doing so, I had traded my past misgivings for a fierce mission in the present: I was determined that my current relationship with my parents would be significantly different from that of the past. Not so hidden was an ambitious agenda: If I could fashion a refurbished relationship with my parents in the present, characterized by compassion and love – give it a makeover, that is – then the wounds of the past would be completely healed. The present would heal the past!

My relationship with my parents did transform in amazing ways. There was much mutual understanding and respect, authenticity and love gained along the way. I continued to have increasing success with my efforts, and it changed my life in many significant ways, until, of course, my approach hit its natural ceiling, its inherent limitation. In spite of my progress, I still carried along a self-concept of 'being wronged,' which remained central to my childhood narrative. And related to this, there remained a fundamental problem: I was still not *choosing* my parents!

I was acting from the premise that I had been dealt a bad hand at birth, and that my adult life was somehow meant to fix this and convert it into a good hand! And while I was making a sincere and wonderful effort to this end, the truth is, until I continued to think of it as a bad hand to begin with, I was still wishing something were different than just the way it was: I was in non-acceptance. Based on my insights about taking responsibility, I wondered: What if I actually *do* have a choice? Could I simply choose these two people as my parents, knowing everything I know about them as human beings? *I declare that forthwith Sushanta Dattagupta and Ranu Dattagupta be chosen as my parents!*

I found that the answer is, "Yes"! I *could* choose them as my parents. (That is when a new definition of forgiveness was revealed to me: forgiveness is not wishing that things are different than they are.) In fact, this effort of choosing what I have subsequently revealed to me in a sudden spark of insight, that *I had indeed chosen them at birth*! In perfect alignment with my soul's purpose in this life, it had made a conscious choice to be born into that particular household, to those particular parents, and at that moment in time!

To take a small deviation here, this insight has matured into the only explanation that makes sense about my physical birth, my experiences thereafter, and my eventual physical death. The apparently random ways in which we take birth or thereafter "have things happen to us," are suddenly not random at all when considered in the eternal flow of energy and matter. As quantum physics explains, physical reality is manifested by the combined collaboration of the observer and the observed. Similarly, our births, which are the physical manifestations of our soul's larger journey, are a unique collaboration between the soul's singular calling in a particular moment and the Universe's context and need in that particular moment. In other words, the soul makes a choice and the Universe makes a choice, and in their unique match in a particular moment in time and space, a physical reality – a life form – is born! [27] Our lives, then, are a sacred 'contract' between the soul and the Universe, but *one that can be rewritten and reshaped along the way through the ongoing exercise of conscious choice!* This writing and rewriting of the contract is at the heart of spiritual creativity, something I take up in considerable depth in the following chapter.

So, returning to choosing my parents at birth, what had appeared all along as not a matter of choice for me, now became clearly of my choosing, and this awareness promptly returned my authentic power. This also meant that cultivating a loving relationship with my parents in the present became an effort free of any burdens or obligations from our shared past. From this point on, I wasn't going to invest in this relationship to heal the past. I was going to do it...*just because*, just because I feel like it, just because it is my choice in this moment.

As you might imagine, this choice began to completely shift the quality of my efforts, and many other positive changes showed up unexpectedly and organically in my relationship with my parents, as well as in our family dynamic. One poignant example is that my self-concept of being the responsible first-born who keeps it all together in the family, quickly disintegrated. As a result, my younger sister was enabled to connect directly with my parents (and vice-versa), and direct more energy to healing and transforming her own independent relationship with them. All this while I had been in the way! So, our family as a collective was able to transcend surviving old and ingrained patterns and launch its first steps into thriving!

While the context of family is a rich example of 'choosing what I have,' this insight is applicable in a variety of situations and can produce extraordinary results. If you love your wife deeply but her mom is not who you would choose for a mother-in-law, you can still choose her as your mother-in-law! If you love your job but one particular aspect of it

---

27. Needless to say, this insight had a profound impact on my entire life perspective. I now knew that everything that had happened thus far in my life – whether apparently 'positive' or 'negative' – had been chosen manifestations to serve my soul's purpose and evolution in this life!

annoys you regularly, you can simply choose that too! If your child is suddenly diagnosed with a learning disability or lifelong disease, the only way to help her is to choose the disability or disease as if you picked it out yourself when you conceived her!

As editors of *Courageous Creativity*, for instance, Shirin and I have developed a conscious practice of actively choosing our contributors once we have agreed that their core idea for an article matches the vision and purpose of our magazine. This means that once past that initial assessment, we work with that person all the way to the end to deliver their article, no matter what. We choose them fully and unequivocally – with their idiosyncrasies, their challenges in timing and delivery, their straying from topic – all of it. And we refuse to stop until their name is in print!

As director of *Yoni ki Baat* in 2011, I practiced the same thing. Once past the five rigorous weeks of story-building through which a self-selected group of participants committed to go on stage with their personal stories, I fully chose each woman for who she was. There was no permission in my heart to wish that anyone was different than just the way she was. In the form of these incredible women, I had been gifted my creative material with all its glorious potential and all its serious limitations. I chose it fully, and I chose to bring out its inherent brilliance!

In this way, 'choosing what I have' goes beyond acceptance and steps into commitment, a topic on which I will share my insights in the final chapter.

I always have a choice

Choice is my ability to say "Just because I do!" beyond and independent of the mental processes of reason and rationality. It is the selection of a path based on what is revealed naturally and organically when I give up mental control – which results in decision making – and submit to my Higher Power.

Choice in action is:

– Intuiting the right path for me, characterized by neutrality towards the available options and by freedom from any urgency or compulsion to go one way or another;

– Pacing myself by inserting space and time, practicing conscious awareness of arising reactivity, and allowing the voice of intuition to emerge;

– Initiating creative action from inner clarity rather than reacting or responding to external circumstances;

– Seeing how I hook challenging or 'negative' external circumstances, and knowing how to unhook, thereby recreating the external circumstances;

– Recognizing that I actually chose what I already have, so to choose it again: actively, consciously, authentically and lovingly.

Recognizing and exercising choice is still a daily practice for me. I'm much more likely to make a choice when I pause and listen to my body and Higher Power for guidance, rather than rely on my mind's calculations and analysis. I know I am making a choice when I connect with what feels right, beyond 'shoulds,' explanations, obligations, laboriousness, compromise, doubt, and guilt. Choice is based on faith, it is fun, and it leaves me content. There is no such thing as a bad choice, though there is such a thing as an inappropriate decision. Choice is the key to a thriving life!

For Guruji

5.

CREATIVITY

Creativity is exercising the power of being in the image and likeness of my Creator. Using pure love as the generative force, spiritual creativity involves consciously harnessing my Higher Power to co-create my life with Her, at every moment.

I create my own life

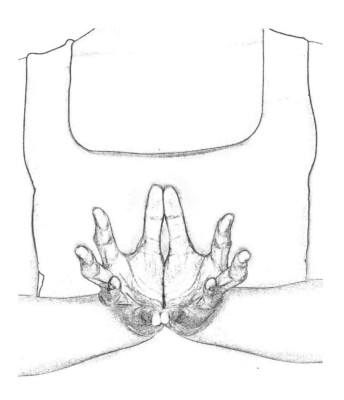

Practicing Authenticity:
Being the [Banyan] Tree

"Your vision will become clear only when you can look into your own heart. Who looks outside, dreams; who looks inside, awakes."

– Carl Jung

Having understood that my life is a sacred contract between my soul and the Universe, one that can be reshaped and rewritten along the way through the ongoing exercise of choice, I began having the inkling that I have the power to *create* my own life. The more my consciousness heightened, the more this insight sharpened into focus: I observed that many of my visions, especially those I believe in with an open heart but without much attachment to the 'how' and 'when' of outcomes, manifest into physical reality! I wondered how I could harness that power consistently, in all areas of my life. I realized that I had to move towards greater authenticity – shed more and more layers and masks of 'what I should be' – and connect instead with 'what I already am,' because that is where my heart is.[28] Because authenticity is the foundation for integrity, which can be defined as the alignment with our true selves, it is also the generative center of original thought and action, which, in turn, is the very definition of creativity.

Like everything else, I found authenticity to be a journey, not a destination. While the insight that there is something 'truer' underneath is an instantaneous realization always already available, the full revelation of that 'truth' is an ongoing process and practice. It continuously reveals itself, as false beliefs from personal, familial, or social conditioning are shed, layer by layer, like a foggy mirror gradually clearing up to reveal one's purest reflection. This process happened for me in fits and starts, and took many a catalyst, starting in 2004 with my twin soul connection with Andrew, and thereafter including several unexpected people and influences along the way.

Sometime in early 2008, my friend and colleague Ana said to a rather frustrated me,

---

28. As Michelangelo is known to have said, his mission as a sculptor was simply to remove the excess stone in a block of marble to reveal the beautiful statue hidden within. Similarly, I needed to become a sculptor with a mission to remove all extra stone to reveal my own truth and singular beauty hidden within.

"You can't be a seedling of a mango tree and turn into an orange tree, you know! You *must* grow into the mango tree!" Ana's words were a startling reminder, yet again, to reconnect with my essence as it progressively revealed itself, and examine if I was being authentic to my Higher Power, and nurturing my highest potential.

By this time I had enjoyed a fabulous, nearly decade-long career with a reputed, global design firm, and had matured into a design strategist, a student of human behavior in the architectural environment, both at the individual level and at the collective level of organizations and communities. *How can we design environments that catalyze human potential?* This was the question that got me out of bed and into the office. I had learned and taught many things, and had amazing opportunities to shape entire courses: of the firm, of clients, and ultimately, of the human beings inhabiting the spaces that we together envisioned, designed and built.

Yet, from day-one I had felt like a gawky misfit in the corporate environment. I couldn't bring myself to sit in a cubicle for eight hours, playing with a mouse or staring at a computer screen, especially if I didn't understand or participate in the bigger picture. I had limited patience for status updates or standing meetings or sitting meetings or state-of-the-firm meetings. I didn't understand corporate politics, or why I was often being asked to change the very attributes that were my strengths in winning projects and clients' hearts, and in doing meaningful work. It appeared that my language was different, my way of seeing and doing things was different, and of course my sociocultural background was different…it seemed that the only way to survive was to chip, chip, chip away at the square peg to fit the round hole. The majority of my time was spent without harnessing the full extent of my energy, intelligence or talents, and instead, was spent fighting to stay in the fray, to swim upstream. What had happened to the little girl who used to paint, sing, stage-act, write, debate, design, dance, play volleyball and run track…? At first I was confused and frustrated, and eventually I became depressed and angry.

Today, insightful and creative education reformers and business minds like Sir Ken Robinson and Seth Godin are urgently reminding us that our education and employment systems continue in the paradigm of the industrial revolution, training us to become units in an assembly line rather than nurturing the seeds of unique talent and potential that are human beings. In many corporate settings, the industrial mindset dangerously masquerades as 'team work,' failing to acknowledge that at the heart of true collaboration is the honoring and celebration of individual singularity and potential, *based on which* appropriate collective synergies can be achieved.[29] As a result, many of us doggedly force-fit ourselves in or devise 'workarounds' to the norm, the givens, the extant circumstances, the round hole. Unfortunately, the cost of forcibly planting oneself in poorly matched soil – whether in work or in relationships – can be huge. It can be the death of a unique, magical seed.

When, among many godsends and signposts came Ana's wise words, I realized I was trying to force myself to become a different tree than of which I was a seedling. So, in mid-2008, I took a three-month sabbatical to participate in a Vipassana meditation course, and to re-engage with my most fundamental gifts. I kept the plan simple: I was going to write, paint and sing. And, I was going to resist my typical inclination to travel, opting instead, to remain grounded in my existing surroundings, in the beautiful summer of Seattle.

In those three months, everything changed, inside and outside. After the ten days of Vipassana – sitting in silence of mind, body and speech – every cell of my body arrived at the clear and unequivocal choice that I must move on from my job. Simultaneously, the economy came crashing down, and when I returned to talk to my employers, I found that my job description, as I had left it, was no longer available. Together we had finally found a 'fit'!

The year 2009 was spent richly reconnecting with my talents and getting a business education, both academically and practically. By the end of that year, I had begun writing prolifically and teaching vocal music, performed in two stage productions, and applied my design strategy skills to social causes. This was a period of committing to daily creativity – through craft, through body, through insight, through service – and through all of this, discovering what it means to make a life before making a living.

It was 2010, however, that really turned the key. Was I gifting my talents enough to really change others' lives? This is the question Seth Godin threw at me in January 2010, through his landmark book, *Linchpin*. Seth reminded me and a zillion others with startling clarity that it is only when you consistently 'ship' the outcome of your creative work, allowing it to interact with audiences, that it is truly relevant. Art isn't art until it takes your personal gift and changes others' lives! I put down *Linchpin* and I made my choice: I was

---

29. One of the managing partners of the firm, whom I had admired and emulated, once admonished me, "Shahana, ours is not a firm of singular stars. We want team players here. No one person can be indispensable!" I remember feeling thoroughly crushed: "What? They don't want me to be the best possible creative that I can be?" It wasn't until I read Seth Godin's *Linchpin: Are You Indispensable?* in 2010, that I felt understood, supported and inspired. It just goes to show that our resonant angels, guides, heroes are everywhere; we just have to trust our inner truths, and they will show up in the outer world!

going to complete my collection of short stories and publish it as a book. Three months of loving labor later, *Ten Avatars* was born. Thus launched my 'writing career,' not by receiving a prize or a grant or permission or a signing bonus, but by making the simple and deliberate choice to connect my art with others.

Many miraculous things rapidly unfolded thereafter. The Seattle community received my work with open hearts, and some of the most poignant and powerful moments came when people told me I had touched their hearts with this story or that one, or that I had inspired them to heed their own true inner callings. There it was, my work interacting with an audience, impacting lives!

By the end of May that year, I already had the urge to make this delight available to others. Inspired by the idea of creating a publishing platform for independent transcultural writers, *Flying Chickadee* was born, in partnership with my friend and collaborator Shirin Subhani. I had always wanted to connect ideas and build something larger than myself: individual creatives with collective synergy. Shirin and I knew that there were many like us, who, in spite of the conditioning of traditional education and employment, had discovered and begun harnessing their essential gifts, and who were willing to share their insights to touch, move and inspire others. And we hoped that the process of telling their stories would nurture these 'seedlings,' as well as spark new seeds. So, we conceived the idea of a small, sharp, beautiful and insightful magazine whose mission is to reveal the courageous paths of those who have recognized their unique gifts or ways of seeing things, and have begun to gift these to the world – in big or small ways. My old colleague – the incredibly creative and socially-entrepreneurial designer, Samuel Stubblefield – joined us in the initiative, and the 'zine *Courageous Creativity* was born in July! Just like that, we began spreading transcultural stories of courage, creativity and change.

In October of the same year, I was invited to direct Seattle's (2011) *Yoni ki Baat*, a powerful and transformative staged show created from a growing repository of original stories of womanhood and sexuality by local South Asian women. (I had been a regular *Yoni ki Baat* participant since its inception in Seattle in 2007.) This gave me an incredible opportunity to translate my extensive participatory design experience from my corporate employment days, to develop a series of story-building workshops for a socially motivated cause. I not only envisioned bringing forth stories that make emotional connections and change lives, but also having the women take responsibility for their own lives, and connect with their creative power. Deeply authentic and powerful storytelling emerged from these workshops, from women who otherwise might not have considered themselves writers. In

March 2011, this process concluded in a weekend of fully sold-out shows at the Seattle Asian Art Museum, receiving standing ovations from about one-thousand people!

Amidst all this, I also received an unexpected call from my old firm's Los Angeles office – the group I had resonated with the most – asking if I would be interested in consulting with them on an international design competition. I got on a plane with three days' notice, and began working on the exciting strategic endeavor, returning to Seattle on weekends for my work with the amazing women of *Yoni ki Baat*. In L.A., it was a delight to work again with some of the most inspiring people I know, and I also observed the marked contrast between my motivation behind doing the work, which was to do the work purely for its own sake, and the outcome-oriented nature of a competitive pursuit. I was able, however, to be still, centered, aware, and connected with my Higher Power. This positively affected others around me, too. I found myself acting as neither an employee nor consultant, but as a mentor and a teacher, and most of all, as a student. I was inspired by others and they by me, and the product we created together represented the unique synergy of all individuals involved. This was true collaboration! [30]

While what emerged from the two meditative and creative years might resemble a career of writing, coaching and consulting, I discovered that the underlying thread through all my work has turned out to have two aspects: acting as a catalyst for others' creative potential, and meaningful storytelling to capture imaginations and change lives. This is true whether I develop the strategy for a design project, write a book, curate and edit *Courageous Creativity*, or direct *Yoni ki Baat*.

Coming full circle to my friend Ana's reminder, perhaps I am a seedling that catalyzes others' creativity, and connects and changes lives through meaningful storytelling. I have always loved the banyan tree. It provides the coolest shade, it is ancient, it takes years to build its wisdom, and as it does so, it reconnects with the very Earth it grows out of, to give back, to take fresh root, to build further connections. It is the tree of enlightenment, the tree under which The Buddha meditated to discover the truth of human suffering. The banyan tree has now become a powerful metaphor for me. I delight in the daily, deliberate, natural and creative process of growing into the tree that I can best be for the world.

---

30. The Los Angeles team went on to win the international design competition, selected over the celebrated Rem Koolhaas and his firm OMA! This work also immediately garnered the firm several other new prospects and design competition invitations in Asia.

It All Starts Within:
In Fractal Relationship to Divine Creativity

"If you are alive, you are creative."

– Patti Digh, *Life is a Verb*

In practicing creativity on a disciplined, daily basis, I suddenly began seeing my multiple talents and inspirations at once as mine, and yet, *not* as mine. On several occasions, while creating something, especially if acting from a place of higher consciousness, I experienced a disintegration of myself as a separate physical being that possesses the particular talent I was exercising. Instead, I experienced my physical self, with all its talents, as a channel for the Muse, in service of a higher purpose, the purpose my soul has come here to fulfill. I got the distinct, tangible feeling that my Higher Power was creating using my physical existence as a channel! [31]

Over time I began to understand that creativity is not just an incidental capability afforded to some, *it is the very purpose* of all human existence! This is because, the Muse *must* flow through human physicality to find expression. I saw with crystal clarity: We are here to create, and creativity is at the heart of thriving!

With the strange and artificial chasm between 'scientific thought' and 'the arts,' creativity has become equated with the latter. Most people do not consider themselves creative, and many a myth has taken over our understanding of creativity. In his book, *The Element: How Finding Your Passion Changes Everything*, Dr. Ken Robinson explores these myths. The first myth, he says, is that only some people are creative. The second is that creativity is about special activities and domains. And the third is that people are either born creative or not. In truth, we are all born with tremendous creative powers, which can be cultivated and exercised, and which can be applied to anything at all we do: managing a company, flying an airplane, raising a child, teaching a class, running a science experiment…or creating one's life itself.

---

31. Recently, I saw a TED Talk on 'Nurturing Creativity' by celebrated author Elizabeth Gilbert, in which she talked about the Muse as an external-to-ego, freely given gift from the Universe, which we neither control nor own; our job as creatives is to do our part in showing up, and just keep doing the work.

One of the most significant and essential attributes of creative thinking or doing is imagination, something everyone possesses but most people rarely tap on a consistent basis. Albert Einstein said, "*Imagination is more important than knowledge.*" I define imagination as the capability for envisioning possibility, without the certainty of proof or validation. When envisioning in this way, creativity moves not only beyond the artistic domains, but also beyond a unique way of doing all work. It becomes the spiritual act of setting into motion the physical manifestation of imagined possibilities. It becomes the act of creating life itself!

Since the power to imagine is innate to us, it follows that creativity too is intrinsic to human consciousness, and its impetus is inside us, not outside us. The seed of the mango tree comes fully equipped with creative intelligence inside it, and it will germinate and grow into the mango tree as soon as it is nurtured with the appropriate soil, nutrients, water and air. Through nurturing my own innate creative seed, I began to have a sense that by accessing her consciousness, the human being can choose to activate her creative seed in a variety of ways, starting by simply imagining possibilities. She is not limited by externalities, and not even particularly by the talents she was or was not gifted at birth. She is limited only by her imagination, her faith, and her ability to follow through with action!

Even when we do dare imagine, not heeding Einstein's insight, we still cede a higher place to 'knowledge,' which is often just dogma. And so, we submit to a limiting system of existence, conveniently calling it 'reality.' We just don't dare to imagine big enough, and we're afraid to create our *own* reality. I often think of all the ridicule the Wright brothers might have faced when they first envisioned flying in the sky like a bird. Undoubtedly, it took incredible imagination, faith and action to realize their dream, transcending collective human doubt as well as the significant 'reality' of gravity and aerodynamics.

Also significantly impeding imagination, faith and action for most humans, is a chronic external orientation. This is the false belief of unidirectional conditionality, expressed simply as, "When X happens, I will be able to do Y." We believe that something is in reach only if and when some enabling factor in the external world shifts, adjusts, or accommodates us, and that such external change must necessarily occur first, before the internal vision can be exercised.

The amazing truth of creative power, which revealed itself to me with continued practice, is that things are quite the other way around! External change (the fruit of creation) is manifested by originating change entirely in one's internal world (the seed of creation). By first envisioning possibility, then by believing in it, and then by acting in accordance with the direction that is organically revealed, imagination manifests into reality. Sir Ken Robinson echoes this in *The Element* when he says, "*The real message [in the concept of creativity] is that we all create and shape the realities of our own lives...*" Robinson goes on to quote William James, one of the founding thinkers of modern psychology: "*The greatest discovery of my generation is that human beings can alter their lives by altering their attitude of mind...if you change your mind, you can change your life.*" This, Robinson suggests, "*is the real power of creativity and the true promise of being in your Element.*"

So, although 'the arts' are the arena in which, like many others, I first started experiencing and practicing my creativity, I soon discovered that at its highest expression, creativity extends to the ultimate frontiers, or rather, to the space of no frontiers. This highest expression I call 'spiritual creativity,' and it extends beyond making things of craft and invention, and even beyond making human organizations and entire movements that transform the world, socially, politically, environmentally and spiritually. At its helm it makes life itself.[32]

One of the unexpected areas of my life in which I was able to practice spiritual creativity is my health. In the first few chapters of this book, I made references to several chronic conditions, such as debilitating migraines, irritable bowel syndrome, a spastic colon, hair loss, tremendous fatigue and painful knees. At some point after I took responsibility and fully embraced the understanding that everything is my choice and my creation, including my illnesses, I was free to imagine a brand new body! I imagined my physical existence as free, strong, active, and thriving.

In fact, over time, it occurred to me how limited we are by the idea that we get older with the passing linear time. Age is more of a mental construct than it is hard physical fact, so, what if I imagined myself growing *younger* with time? This is what I did, and what happened thereafter and how I recovered my health step-by-step through natural means is the subject of a different book altogether. Suffice it to say that I do have a brand new body (albeit a work-in-progress)! Once I imagined this possibility and had faith in my innate capability to heal myself, the right path became illuminated every step of the way, and I was able to take the right actions.

---

32. It is poignant that procreation is an aspect of our creative powers. The power to create physical life is but the starting point of our fuller range of creativity, a hint of what can be!

The continuous practice of spiritual creativity in various aspects of life led me to a momentous epiphany. Just like a fractal structure, in which each sub-aspect, at every progressively lower scale, is in self-similarity with the larger whole, so also divine creativity is in fractal relationship with human creativity! *This* is the meaning of being "created in the likeness of our Creator": At the scale of our existence, each of us has been granted the very same creative powers as our Creator. In a fractal structure, the whole structure supports every fractal level by expressing itself through that level. Similarly, *Creation becomes conscious of itself and expresses itself through human creativity*!

Once I make the connection that I'm made in the likeness of my Creator, anything becomes possible. I see that spiritual creativity is not only my innate divine gift, but that exercising it is my only true life purpose. I, and you – my fellow humans – we are here to create everything: our experiences and our reality, our physical and metaphysical environment, our impacts on others' lives and on the Universe. We are here to create our very lives!

Fear as a Creative Force:
Past Becomes Future without Being Present

"Our deepest fear is not that we are inadequate. Our deepest fear is that we are powerful beyond measure. It is our light that most frightens us. We ask ourselves, "Who am I to be brilliant, gorgeous, talented, fabulous?" Actually, who are you not to be? You are a child of God. Your playing small does not serve the world…"

– Marianne Williamson, *A Return to Love*

So, if we really do create our own lives – moment to moment – how do we do this? And why do we have any so-called 'negative' circumstances at all in our lives? Surely we didn't create *those* too?

That we are creators of our own reality is difficult for most of us to fully embrace because it means taking responsibility at a very fundamental level, for *all* our experiences in life, including those that range from being moderately unfortunate to severely 'negative.' Naturally, it becomes challenging for many of us to accept that we could actually create situations and experiences such as a violent marriage, a damaging friendship, a toxic employment experience, a disastrous client, a severe illness, and so on.

If you're willing, for a moment, to entertain the idea that we are creators of all our experiences, including the so-called negative ones, the first thing to understand is the significant difference between blame and responsibility.

Blame is the idea that we somehow *deserve* the 'bad' things that have happened to us. Blame goes hand-in-hand with unworthiness, shame and secrecy. Our creation of our negative experiences has nothing to do with any value judgment that we 'deserve' these experiences, and it is therefore, free of blame. Responsibility, on the other hand, is the idea that we have a role and a *choice* in every situation no matter what, and that our love for ourselves and for the amazing gift of life behooves us to make the right choice for ourselves. Responsibility goes hand-in-hand with spiritual creativity: We can only harness this power if we take complete responsibility. Thus, blame and responsibility are diametric opposites, and knowing this distinction is exceedingly important in accessing and exercising one's spiritual creativity.

So, the question arises: How can we be responsible for creating negative circumstances and experiences? The answer lies in two related, chronic aspects of typical human existence. The first is the state of being unconscious, and the second is the default outcome of unconsciousness: allowing fear to rule our lives. *Fear is the underlying force behind creating all negative experience,* because it is intrinsically tied to the energy of lack, loss, scarcity and peril. All negative feelings – insecurity, doubt, unworthiness, guilt, resentment, anger, envy, jealousy, hatred – and their associated vibrations, have at their core, fear.

And, in most unconscious moments, *fear becomes the incredibly powerful creative force!* Fear's vibrations put into motion a series of subconscious and unconscious choices on our parts, sending signals to others around us to react with mirroring choices and actions, thus attracting external negativity. As they say, fear begets fear, and so the negative vibrations and related choices continue to exponentially multiply both internally and externally, creating a downward spiral into deeper and deeper levels of negativity.

Because fear is fundamental to survival, it does, of course, serve a purpose. In evolutionary terms, its role is paramount in 'flight-or-fight' situations, such as when we are slipping down a dangerous slope or being attacked by a wild animal. In these moments, fear generates decisive, instinctive reactions to save our lives.

Thriving, however, is neither about reacting nor about preventing death. Thriving is about consciously *creating* our lives. So, when fear begins to extend its influence beyond flight-or-fight situations into our everyday choices and actions, we remain constantly in the survival mindset, and cannot thrive! In this way, survival is antithetic to thriving!

In the chapter Consciousness, I talked about how future becomes past without being present, when we're unconscious and absent to the now. The interesting thing about living unconsciously and allowing fear to drive us is that the opposite is also true: *Past becomes future without being present*! This means that we unconsciously place our pasts in our futures, becoming stuck in the same situations over and over again, as if perennially on a treadmill. When fear rules our lives, we are constantly analyzing and reacting to our past negative experiences, bracing against them and spending all our energy ensuring that they don't repeat themselves, and of course, by the very nature of our focus, they do! It's like driving the car of life looking in the rear-view mirror all the time, and expecting the road to look new or different!

By measuring against the past, we root our desires for the future in reactivity – in "what we *don't* want" – instead of imagining on a blank canvas, what we *do* want! Whenever I've gently posed to any of my friends or those I coach, the simple question: "What do you want?", I've observed how it makes her quite uncomfortable (because she has to take responsibility). It might be met with a straightforward "I don't know!", but more typically it elicits a response in terms of what she *doesn't want*. She might start with, "I want to be happy," but then follow that with, "I just don't want to be so restricted by my financial circumstances anymore," or, "I don't want to be in the same sorry state of health that I've been in in the last five years," or, "I don't want a relationship in which I'm taken for granted all the time," and so on. I've done this myself for the better part of my life, and I cannot emphasize enough, the strong creative power of this kind of thought and language; it places exactly what one *doesn't want*, neatly and squarely in one's future!

In so leading with fear, we become driven by anti-energy – the energy of opposition, of resistance – and we forget to generate *pro-energy*, one that imagines, believes and acts, and thereby, positively creates. We do still create – unconsciously – by allowing fear to be the default creator, attracting more and more of what we don't want into our lives, then reacting with more fear, and so on…keeping the cycle of negativity in perpetual motion.[33] And by continuously placing our pasts in our futures, we have no present (pun intended)!

Love as a Creative Force:
Presence Creates the Future (and the Past)

"The meaning of life is creative love. Not love as an inner feeling, as a private sentimental emotion, but love as a dynamic power moving out in the world and doing something original."

– Tom Morris

Love is the only antidote to fear. Whereas fear is intrinsically tied to a sense of lack and loss, love always knows abundance. So, love is the authentic, conscious force behind all positive creation in and of our lives.

Love is the subject of most books, plays and films from time immemorial, but it continues to intrigue, confuse, elude, and overpower most of us…and by thus being relegated to the domain of emotional life, it remains the most unharnessed power of human existence! To learn to consciously use love as a creative force, one has to first understand what love is. In the chapter on Compassion, I explored what love is not – that "love is not fear." I err on the side of repeating myself here (and throughout the book) on the subject of love, in order to drive home the principal message of this book: True love is the force behind all positive creation.

Since I was a little girl, I have loved openly and frequently, fiercely and fearlessly.

---

33. Entire industries, systems, corporations and governmental operations are created by using fear as the driving force – the insurance industry, the pharmaceutical and drugs industry, the legal system, Homeland Security, "The War on Terror," the education system, the corporate employee evaluation-and-promotion system – all being prime examples.

The vulnerability of love was always terrifying, and yet somehow, I knew innately that an open heart would keep me open to self-discovery and evolution. But it wasn't until I encountered a love that stripped me of any and all remaining masks and left my soul bared in the mirror – in Andrew – that I stumbled into the depths of the meaning and power of love, especially because I experienced a temporary 'loss' in the material plane of this relationship.

It is then that I experienced firsthand that true love starts with loving myself! It demands authenticity and integrity from me at every turn: Once I've seen my soul in the mirror, there is no turning back, no more denying my truth. Being in touch with my essence in this way provides an unexpected access to the larger spiritual be-ing, and in this way, I experience that love is divine. Such unconditional love dispenses of need, promoting a sense of wholeness within: It has immense gratitude for everything just *as it is*. Such love is founded on abundance and courage because it is liberated from concepts of lack or loss: It knows with unerring certainty, its abundant, eternal, non-material existence. Such love is a powerful, radiant flow of energy that can magnetically attract its matching, complementary forces, and create just about anything from nothing. It can bring peace, healing and prosperity in one's own life, in others' lives, and in the world at large. In this way, true, unconditional love is, ultimately, a powerful, transformative, limitless creative force.

By cultivating a meditative stillness in my love for Andrew, I was shown that loving my beloved is the doorway to loving the divine, and *all* other beings. I understood that true love is not just an emotion or feeling, but an action, a persistent, effortful, committed way of being in this world, of doing work and of treating other beings and myself. I also became aware that such love is not reserved just for personal relationships or contexts. It is love, and *only* love – for my clients, colleagues and business partners – that generates meaningful and transformative work, whether as a strategist for architectural and design projects or as an editor of a literary magazine, or as a coach for significant community projects.[34]

As a teacher, it is a deep love for my students, and a seeing and acknowledging of their authentic natures, that makes my music classes not just lessons in music but in life, both for my students and for me. And as a coach, it is an unfaltering and selfless love for the women I guide through transformative storytelling that creates a space of safety and

---

34. Having trouble with this idea? Read *New York Times* Bestseller *Love is the Killer App: How to Win Business and Influence Friends* by Tim Sanders! Other entrepreneurial thinkers and coaches like Dave Pollard, Neil Crofts, and Hugh Macleod have also written on love as a guide for business and enterprise.

trust in which all of us can take risks, be vulnerable, authentic, creative…and transcend surviving to thriving.

Ultimately, love is the generative force behind all my artistic and spiritual creativity, my very raison d'être. And to truly love means to create and let go, create and let go…This constant vulnerability is what successfully and positively creates life. Because every action is in highest consciousness and motivated only by pure love – positive intention, abundance, grace, authenticity, vulnerability, courage and spirit – *the future is created in the present*, rather than as a reaction to the past.

What's more, by loving in this way, I can also enable *the present to (re)create the past*! Living and acting with love makes it impossible to view my past with negativity, bitterness, guilt or regret, and therefore, it fundamentally changes my relationship with my past. A new view, a new story of the past becomes possible, which is authentic to who I am in the present. Since the only place the past exists is in my memory and in my own stories about it, this reorientation is tantamount to recreating the past!

Loving and creating in this way isn't always easy; it is indeed a challenging, daily spiritual exercise, a channel for constant growth, and an ongoing, deepening dialogue with the divine. Fear, the other side of the coin, is always ready to topple the delicate balance. It is impossible to be fearless because fear serves a purpose, and it remains a lurking shadow in every human being's existence. The alternative to being fearful is, therefore, not being fearless, but *being courageous*. As has been aptly said, courage is not the absence of fear, but acting in spite of it. Courage is the ability to act from the strength of the heart, that is, to act with love.[35] This requires gentleness and compassion towards oneself every time one falls prey to fear, and it demands strength, determination and faith to return, always and without fail, to love.

While it is challenging, loving and creating in this way is tremendously joyful and liberating. It opens the door to the mysterious magic of life, to a landscape of endless possibilities, and to an abundant, limitless power for inner and outer transformation. It makes me thrive!

---

35. The word 'courage' comes from the Latin 'cor' and the French 'coer,' both of which mean some combination of heart and spirit.

Unlocking Creative Power:
Wholeness, Abundance, Gratitude and Resonance

"You have to participate relentlessly in the manifestation of your own blessings."

– Elizabeth Gilbert, *Eat, Pray, Love*

As I recognized love as the supreme, positive, divine force behind my creative power, I began experiencing a state of being and creating characterized by feelings of wholeness and integration, abundance and gratitude. This state of being put me in growing resonance with my Higher Power, and I was able to do Her bidding to consistently create loving outcomes.

Then I discovered that these feelings, which are essentially facets of love, have been taught as spiritual principles by many masters and traditions over the centuries of human existence, in various ways and using varying language. What I share here is based on my direct, experiential discovery, informed by the teachings and insights of various teachers, which I drew organically into my awareness along the way.

The spiritual principles that unlock spiritual creativity and enable it to realize its full expression are: *Wholeness*, *Abundance*, *Gratitude*, and *Resonance*.

The first spiritual principle, *Wholeness,* is the peaceful, unerring knowing that I am whole and complete just as-is. While I may appear to need other people, relationships, material objects, or external circumstances to support my material existence and my undertakings of physically manifest work, none of these things are necessary for my essential, spiritual existence. In my true nature, at the level of my soul, *I am already complete and whole at all times*. My physical, emotional and intellectual existence serves as a playground, a stage, a construction site, to remind me of this fact, and always return me to my true nature.

When I first landed on this, it seemed like a simple and straightforward understanding to maintain, but in practice, we are chronically driven by things outside of ourselves to feel complete and whole in our daily living. As I described in the chapter Centering, the visceral connection with my own 'center of gravity' was powerful in revealing my *Wholeness*, and this bodily reminder continues to serve me to this day whenever I topple out of balance. Another constant teacher is the incredible experience of seeing my truer nature reflected in Andrew, and remaining conscious that this is a reflection of my *own Wholeness*, rather than defaulting to an unconscious reliance on him to 'complete me'! In this way, *Wholeness* is an aspect of true love, because true love comes from a complete, open, and authentically powerful heart, in full awareness and acceptance of *what is*, and no fear of depletion or incompletion.

The second spiritual principle, *Abundance*, I find, is the happy complement of *Wholeness*. It is the faith that while I am already spiritually whole, all that I do need for my material sustenance – whether physical, emotional or intellectual – will unfailingly and always be provided by the Universe. I discovered that paradoxically, it is only when I am fully comfortable in my *Wholeness,* that I trigger material abundance to enter, and even flood my life!

This faith in *Abundance* means that I must have equanimity in events ranging from the stinginess of a friend to the global economic recession. I must know, even in seemingly dire circumstances and even when there's no light visible at the end of the tunnel, that I have enough and I will always have enough. (I can assure you that without this faith I couldn't have put aside everything to write this book!) *Abundance* is an aspect of true love because a complete, open and authentically powerful heart knows that it is a bountiful and limitless wellspring of love and creativity. There is no dearth, no beginning, and no end to its love.

The third spiritual principle is *Gratitude*, also a much exalted attitude in New Age philosophy and Yogic practices. *Gratitude* is the vibrational quality of being in constant thanksgiving. I see it as the natural third-wheel along with *Wholeness* and *Abundance*: When I know with constant certainty my wholeness, and I know the Universe's gift of abundance, then I am bound to be grateful all the time.

Gratitude means that without having to make a concerted effort, I habitually and naturally see the silver lining in every situation, always recognize the opportunity for soul work in apparent adversity, and always make (more than) lemonade from lemons, all the while being delighted for these hidden gifts! *Gratitude* is an aspect of true love because a complete, open and authentically powerful heart knows it already has everything it needs, and its natural state is one of constant appreciation and thanksgiving.

So, *Wholeness, Abundance* and *Gratitude*, as aspects of true love, make a sturdy triad for the foundation of my spiritual creativity. The fourth principle, *Resonance*, is a way of relating and engaging with the world, and a natural outcome of practicing the three principles.

Resonance is the state of being completely in tune, harmony and collaboration with the other positive, creative forces in the Universe. Many teachers have talked about *The Law of Attraction*, teaching that we always attract all our experiences – both positive and negative – as an exact mirror of our own internal energetic quality. While attraction explains the magnetic power hidden in our inner core, *Resonance* as a principle reminds me that this attraction is a two-way street, representative of my sacred contract with the Universe. I send *and* receive energy, and it is through this two-way energetic exchange with the Universe that my life is co-created, whether consciously or unconsciously. Being in *Resonance* means I can consciously employ love and all its aspects to attract the aid of positive, creative forces in the Universe, thereby co-creating my life with them.

By knowing and remaining connected to the aspects of love – *Wholeness, Abundance* and *Gratitude* – invoking *Resonance* becomes second nature, and I can consciously replace the default of unconscious, fear-based creation. When I am in conscious, positive, creative resonance with the Universe – that is, the vibrational quality 'in here' matches or complements something 'out there' – I am able to create positive reality all the time!

Exercising Creative Power:
I Imagine, I Make, I Interact

"Imagination is the beginning of creation. You imagine what you desire, you will what you imagine and at last you create what you will."

– George Bernard Shaw

Having understood the principles for unlocking my spiritual creativity – *Wholeness, Abundance, Gratitude* and *Resonance* – I began practicing it in various life contexts, such as the trajectory of my consulting projects, my endeavors with the *Flying Chickadee* publishing platform, writing and teaching music, my physical and financial health, my friendships and relationships, and so on. Gradually, I homed in to an approach to exercising spiritual creativity that can be applied to any life context!

Although the mistaken relegation of creativity to the domain of the arts undermines the full extent of human creative potential, this domain did, nevertheless, hold the key to my significant discoveries about exercising the full power of creativity. As I practiced creativity through avenues such as visual art, music, architecture, and writing, I stumbled upon an important insight: There are clear practical parallels in exercising artistic creativity and spiritual creativity. I discovered that the same practical methods and approaches that are involved in the making of powerful objects of art that touch, move and inspire others, can be translated to the practice of spiritual creativity, which generates life and all its circumstances, experiences and outcomes!

As I mentioned before, imagination, faith and action are three vital components of any creative exercise. Faith is established by practicing the spiritual principles of *Wholeness*, *Abundance*, *Gratitude* and *Resonance*, and action can be expanded into two components: making and interacting. So, assuming a foundation of faith, the approach to exercising creativity is *Imagining-Making-Interacting*, and one way to express its spiritual translation is *Asking-Visualizing-Receiving*. [36]

The first act of creation is *Imagining*, whether it be a product, event or an outcome. Without imagination life would continue just as it always has, only because we could imagine no differently. The step of imagining freely, just because, without reservation or judgment about how or when an idea can be realized, is the very genesis of creation. Imagining in this way requires me to have pure, unfettered, childlike faith that anything is possible. It is spirited, uplifting and joyous, and opens up naturally when I am in *Resonance*. There is little room for self-doubt, second-guessing, or fear: I must imagine wholeheartedly, with courage and with love.

The spiritual translation of this step is *Asking* – simply making a request of the Universe – for that which I have imagined. This request, as suggested earlier, must be made

---

36. The bestselling and controversial book *The Secret* by Rhonda Byrnes proposes a model of Ask-Believe-Receive. I am deeply grateful for the framework Byrnes provided through her book; by borrowing and adapting her framework I am able to concisely describe the insights that I gained in my own spiritual journey.

free of reservations or judgment, and free of concerns over how or when it will be granted. All I must do, I find, is to freely imagine and ask, and know that it will be granted.

The next act of creation is *Making*. When working on an artistic product that is tangibly physical, this means to actually go about building it: mocking it up, iterating through innovations, and then completing it with discipline. In this process of making, I've found it effective to develop project-based 'dreamlines,' which are dedicated three- to six-month periods, at the end of which the particular creative project will be completed and ready to share with an audience. The act of making must be disciplined, consistent and regular, preferably every single day! For making to manifest in a successful product, event or outcome, it must be undertaken with feelings of joy and exhilaration. It just *has* to be fun!

The spiritual translation of physical making is *Visualizing*. Whatever is imagined and asked for is now visualized with unflinching faith *as if it were already true*. Like the physical making process, this is also accompanied with the joy, exhilaration and gratitude associated with a dream already realized in form. For such visualizing, it helps to place myself in parallel situations and circumstances that generate the feelings and internal disposition associated with the dream-come-true. Generating such feelings is easy when I am grateful for what I already have, or when I see others who are successful in something analogous to what I wish for myself, and feel genuine elation for them.

Another way of visualizing is to physically make something, just like I would in the artistic creative process. This kind of making might involve things like a vision board, a purpose statement, or a piece of art or writing that expresses a dream-come-true. In their moving book, *The Art of Possibility*, Benjamin Zander, Boston Philharmonic conductor and a leading interpreter of Mahler and Beethoven, and his wife Rosamund Stone Zander, a family therapist and executive coach, describe just such a making exercise, which they call 'Giving an A.' All Benjamin's students receive an A at the outset of his course! The only requirement is that they write a letter to Benjamin dated a year into the future, constructed in past-tense and looking back to the present, describing explicitly how they will have re-invented themselves as creative beings, (including any milestones and accomplishments they will have achieved), through the yearlong course. This extraordinary act invites Benjamin's students to the possibility of inventing new futures simply by imagining and making in the present; in other words, they become free to *create* themselves and their futures!

Undertaking a similar exercise in late 2008, I worked through a process of self-discovery proposed by Dave Pollard in his transformative book *Finding the Sweet Spot*, and I arrived at a purpose statement for myself: *To be a catalyst for others' highest creative potential through the exercise of my own.* I wrote this out in large letters and pinned it up above my desk, where I could see it every day. I often smiled with the intention, passion and conviction of the words. By envisioning and inventing my role in the world, all my actions and endeavors began to align themselves with this vision, and those that didn't, began to naturally fall away. Down the road, I was inspired to rigorously ensure that *every single project* I undertake – no matter the talent or skill it engages and its financial potential – fulfill both requirements in the statement! By 2011, the statement came fully to life through at least four endeavors: *Courageous Creativity*, *Yoni ki Baat*, teaching classical music, creativity coaching, and design consulting!

The final act of creation is *Interacting*. In the domain of physical making, although the creative product itself might be 'complete' at the making stage, the greater act of creation is left incomplete if the product, event or outcome is not vulnerably offered to an audience for mutual interaction and enrichment. It must have an opportunity to touch, move and inspire others, as well as to provide the creator with feedback and inspiration for further creativity. By definition, then, this is a two-way exchange, allowing the creator to receive generative input through the act of giving, sharing and interacting.

So, for example, if I have completed a series of paintings, these must go beyond standing in a stack in my studio or even hanging on the walls of my home, to be shared with a larger number of people through publication on a Web site, or physical display in an exhibition. If I have written an insightful essay, it must make its way into my blog, or into a published book. If I've learned a beautiful composition it must be taught to others, or offered as a performance in relevant gatherings. These acts of sharing and interacting don't have to be monumental: *Every little act counts.*

The spiritual translation of interacting is *Receiving*: It is an interaction with the Universe. This is the step in which an imagined and visualized outcome manifests into reality. The Universe offers unique opportunities in the form of signs, situations, people, or resources. My job is to recognize these, and then act promptly and unequivocally. I must be able and prepared to receive these gifts, without hesitation, doubt or fear. I've found that a good way to recognize these gifts, especially when I am in *Resonance* with the Universe, is knowing that they typically arrive rapidly, naturally and freely, without much straining or pursuing on my part. They are often experienced as serendipitous and organic events, and they leave me with feelings of awe, wonderment, joy and gratitude. Time feels non-linear, and sometimes stands still altogether, and it is easy to forget myself. When I am feeling this way, it is certain that I have manifested into reality, what I have imagined and asked for!

Completing the Creative Cycle:
The Art of Receiving

"As far as inner transformation is concerned, you cannot transform yourself or anybody else. All you CAN do is create a space for transformation to happen, for grace and love to enter."

– Eckhart Tolle, *The Power of Now*

Because *Receiving* is the significant final act in spiritual creativity, during which an imagined and envisioned outcome manifests into physical reality, it is worth exploring our conditioned difficulties with it. The 'art of giving' and its virtues have been much extolled, but over the course of the last seven years, my insights about the 'art of receiving' have significantly transformed my worldview, interactions and relationships. They have strengthened my ability to harness my creative power and manifest positive reality.

Terms such as 'give and take' create the indelible impression that the opposite of 'giving' must necessarily be 'taking,' labeling the interaction as a mere transaction. In truth, however, any generous, conscious act of giving must be accompanied and complemented by an equally generous, conscious act of receiving, or it becomes a block in the flow of the Universe.

My earliest insights on this came on the massage table, working with my gifted therapist and Reiki specialist, David. Initially, of course, it had seemed to me that David was doing all the work, while I lay passively on the table, often dozing off. Over time, as my body began to recognize and open up more fully to David's healing touch and energy work, I noticed that my attitude, intentions, openness, and frame of mind as I lay on the table greatly impacted the benefits I experienced from the session. Eventually, when David practiced Reiki with me, I was able to palpably feel the energy course through my body, like a warm river, beginning with my head and 'leaving' through the soles of my feet. And whenever I actively and consciously tuned in to receive David's Reiki, the tangible experience of these energetic vibrations was greatly enhanced. I realized that all of David's hard work would translate into real benefits only if I also did the hard work of consciously, actively, and appropriately receiving it.

The next insights in the art of receiving came when I took a course in Vipassana meditation with the Northwest center of the Goenka School. The entire course was free of cost, including ten days of instruction, room-and-board, and food! If, on completing the course, one has the willingness and ability, one may donate an amount of one's choosing, so that someone else may also get the gift one just received! Two things struck me about this arrangement. First, *I was receiving the gift of someone else's generosity*, and second, *I couldn't look at the experience as a transactional exchange*, in which I paid someone an amount and they gave me something in return. The Vipassana Center owed me nothing. (I couldn't use money as an excuse to not do the course in the first place.) Instead, I owed it to myself to work hard, and to complete the physically, emotionally and spiritually challenging endeavor. In other words, receiving this amazing gift was hard work!

The exact same thing is true each time my beloved Guru, Pandita Tripti Mukherjee, hosts me for several days in her *Gurukul* [37] in New York, and teaches me Indian classical music (along with much life wisdom). Receiving her divine gift involves sincere, hard work, because our interaction transcends transaction. No amount of monetary payment could ever cover her gift, and so, the highest and best I can do is to learn and practice with diligence, and to share this treasured and ancient art with others.

My insights about receiving in these different contexts had me reflecting on 'the art of receiving' in general. I had always enjoyed giving gifts, often with great care, thoughtfulness and generosity. I loved to surprise my loved ones with handmade cards, parties, presents or travel arrangements. But when it came to getting gifts or favors, I often turned bashful, embarrassed and reluctant to accept them, especially if it involved money, (partly due to my upbringing, and partly due to the cultural emphasis placed on 'giving unselfishly').

---

37. A *Gurukul* is a traditional Indian school, residential in nature, with *shishyas* (disciples) living in proximity to the Guru, often within the same house. In a *Gurukul*, *shishyas* reside together as equals, irrespective of their social standing, learn from the Guru and help her in her day-to-day life, including the carrying out of chores and tasks related to the school and home.

And if I did accept someone's help or birthday present or treat to dinner, I'd quickly be thinking about how to return the favor. In other words, I'd be looking to circumvent the actual work of graceful receiving, opting for the easier path of converting the interaction into a transactional exchange.

Now I began to see that being comfortable with giving but not with receiving is, paradoxically, egocentric and selfish, and interferes with creating positive outcomes! Receiving the Universe's gifts requires grace, effort and accountability. It behooves me to step up to the gift as its deserving recipient! It requires me to understand that making the most of someone's gift is the best way to honor their effort and generosity. In everyday terms, this means that if someone invites me to dinner at their home, I attend with presence, I savor every bite, I cherish every conversation, I remember everyone's names. (In other words, I practice consciousness.) The easier path would be to insist on bringing dessert, or a present, or flowers to return my host's favor, and walk away assured that I've paid my dues.[38] It also means that if someone gifts me a pair of earrings, I (skip the gratuitous thank-you card and) actually wear the earrings the next time I see her, and share my genuine enjoyment and appreciation. And it means that when someone, such as my Guru, teaches me something, (I defocus from how I'll be returning her favor and) I pay attention, learn well, and apply her guidance and advice to make positive change in my life and in the lives of others. And most of all, when someone gives me his genuine love, I allow it to shine light into my life.

This way of receiving has enhanced my understanding of true giving as well. "What goes around comes around" really means that giving into the Universe with love and receiving from the Universe with love, together create a constant cycle, and *both* are necessary to keep the flow going. As my friend Bipasha once said to me, "Generosity is complete only when the receiver receives with as much generosity as with which the giver gives." So, it is important to practice the art of receiving just as well as the art of giving.

A significant aspect of this final act of creation is that it is best done by consciously, lovingly and humbly *making space* for freely given gifts of grace, which requires inner work and preparation. Receiving is not a relentless, obsessive or greedy pursuit of a want. Instead, it is a brimming awareness that what has been asked for will be freely gifted when it is in positive resonance with Universal order. This ultimate insight in the art of receiving

---

38. Of course, if the dessert came on top of my non-material efforts, it would be part of graceful and effortful receiving!

came to me through learning (and teaching) the difficult and complex art form of Indian classical music. I discovered that while hard work and diligence are requirements, they are neither sufficient nor necessarily progressive in impact. I have to show up and do the hard work, but without expectation of return, and be open instead, to receiving sudden and unexpected gifts of insight and understanding at any moment!

For instance, getting even a mere footing in the complex form of the *bada khayal*,[39] has taken me years. When clarity did come, however, it arrived in an instant: unannounced, unexpected, and in a quantum leap. In that discernible and memorable moment, my class recordings were playing in the background while I was creating one of my larger acrylic-on-canvas paintings. (I had previously listened to and practiced along with these recordings countless times.) My brush was moving meditatively on the large canvas, and suddenly, the fog lifted. What I hadn't been able to comprehend for years clicked into place in one instant, and I suddenly began singing *bada khayal* in *Raga Alhaiyya Bilaval* as if I had been practicing it for several months at a stretch (which I had not). It was now that I understood the significance of the traditional ritual of invoking the permission and blessings of one's elders, Guru, and the divine before learning or performing this ancient musical form. This is the act of *Asking* in the spiritual creation process, a conscious opening of oneself to receiving musical and spiritual insight. Creating and receiving, hand in hand!

And this is also why, I realize, there is an emphasis in some religions on attaining 'heaven' solely through submitting oneself without question to divine guidance, rather than through one's moral 'hard work.' It is the difference between gracefully and humbly making space for welcoming a gift, and hotly and doggedly pursuing something. It is only when I am liberated from notions of 'hard work' and a sense of entitlement around its expected returns, and become open to receiving freely given gifts of insight and guidance from my Higher Power, that I truly harness my ability to create my life: not in a future heaven, but right here, right now!

---

39. The *bada khayal* is a compositional form of presenting *Ragas*: the complex melodic structures with frameworks of rules that form the basis of Indian classical music. While the *Raga* itself is adequately complex to learn and present, the *bada khayal* form uses a particular type of rhythm cycle that further intensifies the complexity of the presentation, requiring the artiste to improvise with both melody and rhythm in real time, to part ways with and rejoin the rhythmic cycle in 'grammatically' correct ways.

CREATIVITY

I create my own life

Creativity is the ability to consciously harness the power I innately possess to create my own reality and life. Spiritual creativity has close parallels with artistic creativity, and can be exercised in analogous ways.

Creativity in action is:

— Moving towards greater authenticity, by progressively shedding more layers and masks of 'what I should be,' and connecting with 'what I already am';

— Recognizing that the power to invent our own lives is in fractal relationship with divine creativity;

— Becoming conscious to fear, which is the default creative force, due to which we root our desires for the future in "what we *don't* want," and become driven by anti-energy, the energy of opposition, of resistance;

— Connecting with true love as the only generative, positive, all-powerful creative force, that allows us to imagine on a blank canvas what we *do* want;

— Cultivating the spiritual principles of *Wholeness, Abundance, Gratitude* and *Resonance,* which are, essentially, aspects of true love;

— Exercising the triad of *Imagining-Making-Interacting*, and its spiritual correspondent *Asking-Envisioning-Receiving*;

— Receiving the Universe's gifts with grace, effort and accountability.

The meaning of being in the image and likeness of my Creator is that I become a co-creator of this life with Her, fulfilling my sacred contract with the Universe. Therefore, *creativity is the purpose of life*. It is at the very heart of thriving!

For Sabina

6.
CONNECTEDNESS

Connectedness is the awareness that I am a part of a bigger whole, and that what is outside myself is a reflection of what is inside myself. It is the knowing that every good and every evil is at once out there and in here, and that each action really does have a corresponding reaction somewhere in our connected, collective existence.

I am all, all are me

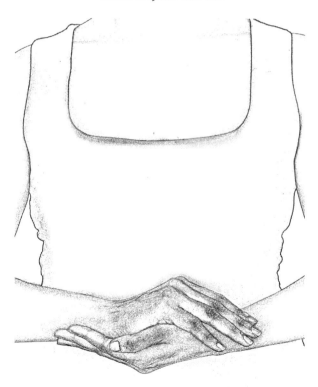

Connectedness Within:
Shared Earth and Shared Oxygen

"When we try to pick out anything by itself, we find it hitched to everything else in the Universe."

– John Muir

In becoming more adept at practicing consciousness, as well as accessing and exercising my spiritual creativity, an overarching, enveloping sense of connectedness began to govern my life and actions. The experience of connectedness arrived in multiple layers in a somewhat order-less, scale-less way. What I first experienced as a mysterious, telepathic connectedness with Andrew, led me unexpectedly to the divine, and then brought me full circle to my own inner self, wherein previously isolated aspects began to rapidly connect with each other. As this happened, I quickly saw the unmistakable, direct connectedness between my internal energy state and the external 'reality' in my life, which further revealed to me, the connectedness between me and all other beings. This was then followed by the understanding of connectedness not only at the macro scale – in and between entire communities, countries, planets, and galaxies – but also between all energy and particles at the micro scale.

At the personal level, a common means of survival at which humans become adept over time is a compartmentalization of various aspects of themselves and their lives. I like to call this the 'potted plants' way of living. We believe that by organizing and ordering our lives into various pots, we can nurture each separately, perhaps more safely and competently. So, our career is in one pot and our personal life in another pot. Our social lives are in different pots: the professional kind and the personal kind. Our financial status is in one pot, our health in a different pot, and the types of friends and associations we keep in yet another pot. The quality of our intimate relationships is in one pot, and the performance of our children in school is in a different pot. The aspects we present at home and outside are in separate pots, as are those we present as parents of our children or children of our parents…and so on. And we want desperately for these worlds never to mix! In each pot grows, we believe, a different species of plant with its own particular needs and qualities, so we tend to each of these accordingly, with customized care.

This kind of compartmentalization may serve us in the short-term because it helps us operationally, to function more easily, to feel comfortable and safe in negotiating life in smaller chunks. *It helps in our survival.* At some point, however, the division can become so extreme that we lose our integrity, our sense of wholeness and oneness, both within ourselves and with the Universe. *It doesn't allow us to thrive.*

We forget that all the pots contain the same earth, and that all the plants breathe the same oxygen: the earth and oxygen of one's whole energetic existence. We are blind to the insight that it is the toxicity or health at the integrated level of 'one-self' that drives the quality of all our potted plants and their potential to prosper and thrive, not merely survive. On the flip side, we also miss seeing that toxicity or health in one pot affects and changes the earth and oxygen for all our pots.

Imagine, instead, a life of continuous, connected fields of luscious green. When we remember and reconnect with our whole energetic existence, we can make shifts at the meta-level that affect all our life-aspects, individually and combined.

In mid-2010, in my work as a design strategy consultant, I came within inches of working on a number of promising projects. Repeatedly, however, they kept from materializing, even after threatening to launch 'tomorrow.' I felt stuck in a frustrating limbo. After a brief period of struggle with the leads, I let go, and zoomed out to the larger field of green. Instantly, I saw that an overarching energy of 'limbo' characterized some other things I was doing (or not doing) in my life: a lingering ambiguity in my relationship status with Jason even after several months of having 'broken up,' a lack of clarity in my housing situation, several unfinished creative or home projects, momentary indecision about accepting the director's role I was offered in Seattle's *Yoni ki Baat*, and a few other unmet or overpromised commitments. In that moment of realization, I also saw that I, as one-self, was *generating* the energy of limbo – of indecision and non-commitment – and that this was therefore the current energetic quality of my existence as a whole, not simply an issue inside the consulting 'pot.'

I've observed and witnessed others get stuck in similar overarching energetic places, usually somehow related to their deeper limiting beliefs about themselves or their life experiences. For one, it is the energy of low self-esteem or confidence, and for another, it is one of loneliness or abandonment. For one, it is energy of victimization, and for yet another, it is one of envy or competitiveness. These individuals may believe they are stuck in one 'pot' of their lives, and struggle to overcome issues within that aspect, but they are missing the bigger picture – the whole green field – the level at which transformation can best occur. So, they continue to attract the same energetic experiences, which confirm their beliefs about the world and themselves, and thus repeatedly reinforce their negative inner energy-state.

The corollary to the belief that compartmentalization serves us well, is the belief that something outside of us first needs fixing, for things to change. In the chapter Creativity, I noted that humans often fall prey to the notion: "When X happens, I will be able to do Y," which is the belief that something is out of reach until something else in the external world shifts, adjusts, or accommodates us. In my example of being stuck with consulting prospects, such a belief would translate to: "If only the companies I am consulting with would get their act together and stop being so wishy-washy about what they want, then I'd be working on these wonderful projects pronto!"

Once I saw the truth that my inner energetic state not only matches but actually *creates* my external reality, I knew that I could generate the required energetic change within me, and thereby shift the external milieu to reflect and match my new energy. In other words, in order for the consulting prospects to become unstuck, I would need to convert my fear-based, non-committal inner energy to a love-based energy of positive commitment.

As an aside, a significant and much worried about 'potted' aspect of life in which the phenomenon of inner energetic state creating external reality manifests for most of us is the green stuff: money. With an increasing sense of connectedness, I quickly discovered that my financial health is more an energetic state of being, and less the strength or volume of my bank account. If my energetic state is one of lack, then quickly, the 'reality' of my resources will reflect this. If my energetic state is one of abundance, then too my resources will reflect this. Like love, money is essentially a form of energy, and behaves as such. Spending, sharing and giving it with positive, love-based energy keeps it freely flowing through us, while hoarding it with fear-based energy erects a dam, preventing any more from coming through!

These insights led me to take concrete steps to transform my state of limbo into one of positive action. For one, I realized that a significant change was required in the one aspect of my life in which I was exhibiting the largest indecision and non-commitment: my relationship status with Jason. So, I chose to immediately get greater clarity in it, which in this case involved firmly and unequivocally reframing our relationship as a friendship, one in which any lingering romantic expectations were fully relinquished.[40] Despite considerable struggle to create and exercise new boundaries, taking this important step instantly and dramatically transformed my overall energy, and thereby all other life aspects.

Next, I reviewed all lingering commitments or projects that, in all honesty, I was not authentically passionate about, and simply eliminated them. Finally, I wholeheartedly and unequivocally committed to those things that I am passionate about – projects, causes, relationships – and chose to follow through completely. I resumed working on this book, dived with heart-and-soul into directing *Yoni ki Baat* to work with the largest turnout of participants in its five-year history in Seattle, and completed several paintings. I also set a firm date with my renter to move back into my condominium unit in downtown Seattle, instead of succumbing to my falling courage and making half-hearted attempts to sell it. And lo and behold! By the end of the year, the opportunity to consult on a significant project involving an international design competition materialized as if out of thin air!

By breaking down the artificial walls of the potted plants and viewing my life as a continuous green field with shared earth and shared oxygen, I was able to breathe new energy into it as a whole. By fully embracing inner and outer connectedness, I was able to connect and resonate with the Universe, enabling the right, matching opportunities to come my way naturally and organically. Simply by generating a different energy from within – one of conscious choice and authentic commitment – I successfully reshaped my external reality.

---

40. Commitment in a romantic relationship is commonly defined as one's wholeheartedness and tenacity to remain in it, resulting, it is typically hoped, in quality and longevity. I found, however, that when a romantic relationship is clearly dissonant and no longer productive to one's (spiritual and creative) evolution, being unequivocal about the 'break-up' is *also* a form of commitment! More on commitment in the final chapter.

The Myth of Separateness:
I am He and He is I!

"If I truly love one person I love all persons, I love the world, I love life. If I can say to some-body else, "I love you," I must be able to say, "I love in you everybody, I love through you the world, I love in you also myself."

– Erich Fromm, *The Art of Loving*

With growing internal integrity and oneness within, came the powerful and moving experience of being on a seamless continuum with the external world. I began see-ing visions of myself as an energetic continuation of other beings around me, rather than as a separate and distinct entity that my physicality implies.

A particular repetitive occurrence that created these visions was my running into any of the poverty-ridden, stench-engulfed homeless people on the street right outside my condominium building in downtown Seattle. Sometimes they were sitting around or ambling along, and at other times, openly swapping drugs for change near the garbage dumpsters in the back alley. My initial, instinctive and visceral responses to the grime and crime were ones of sadness and disapproval, respectively. "I could be him!" I would think, with genuine feeling. These reactions, however, were still characterized by separateness: That is he, the stinky homeless man, and this is I, the woman who lives on the sixth floor with her view of Mt. Rainier, capable of empathizing with him, but also of shutting him out with the push of a button on the garage device in her glove compartment. Our lives were separated by more than building walls and garage doors; we were distinct and separate beings altogether.

With every encounter though, I unwittingly began having palpable experiences of the edges of my separate existence blurring out, resulting in seeing myself both in his shoes *and* in my own. 'I' was at once the guy in tatters, lugging around some semblance of be-longings, as well as the woman in fancy clothes, pulling into the parking garage and taking the elevator up to the sixth floor. In the language of quantum physics, my soul could have two probabilistic tendencies. Instead of "I could be him!" the message resonating through me in these visions and experiences was: "I *am* he and he *is* I!"

In these moments, I could feel my heart cracking open. *This* must be love in action: a discernible feeling of energy being transmitted from my heart to his, and energy received by my heart from his, transcending all the formidable boundaries that separated us, flowing freely in spite of all the visible discomfort and distance. In these fleeting instants, there was a tangible thread connecting our souls, and we were, suddenly, one organism, one unified being. It wasn't my place to evaluate his position to be any worse than mine, or even to 'empathize' with him. All I had to do is simply experience, hold and embrace the truth that *we are one*. I knew then what philosophers, metaphysicists and spiritual gurus are referring to when they say that duality is the illusion of human existence. They are alluding to the seamless unity I experienced in those amazing, fortunate, gifting moments.

The next profound and revealing experience came during my first ten-day Vipassana meditation course in 2008, which reinforced my understanding further. For the first three days all we did was observe the sensations produced by our breaths falling on the little triangular portion between our noses and upper lips. But on the fourth day, when we were instructed to carry our newly sharpened observation capability to the rest of our bodies, I began feeling sensations I had never known even existed in my body, sometimes on the surface, at other times deep inside, sometimes hot, at others cold, sometimes mild and fleeting, at others gross and heavy…and it all changed constantly and eternally. By the eighth day, I felt these sensations so acutely that they were reduced to finer energetic vibrations instead of more solid, aggregated feelings, until ultimately, I had the experience of the hard edges of my body dissolving and becoming one with everything around me. That is when I knew with utter certainty – through tangible bodily experience – the truth that I am connected to all and all are connected to me.

Other visions reinforcing this truth were those in which all the people in my life merged into one unified being. For instance, I had flashes of seeing certain essential qualities and characteristics of all the significant men who have been in my life, as if they were of the very same being: a unified male essence. They appeared now as varied aspects, facets, expressions, avatars…of the same kernel of masculine energy, traceable to the complementary feminine energy in me. So, for all the singularity of Andrew in my life, it was startling and amazing to experience that distilled to a spiritual essence, he is at once singularly he and also in unity with the others: an expression of the divine One!

Through these flashes of knowing oneness, I also saw the powerful truth that because love manifests for me in its most resonant and highest avatar in my twin-soul relationship with Andrew, this particular love is a heightened expression of my capability for

Universal love, including love for all other beings, for all the men who have been before and since, be it my love-interests in school or college, or my ex-husband, or later, Jason. My love for Andrew is singular to him, and at the same time it is offered to all. My love for him is also my love for myself, and ultimately, it is my love for the divine. This oneness of love and the corresponding oneness of all beings is the closest tangible and visceral experience I've had to understanding the divine, the absolute, The One. And I understood that love *is* the divine: It is both the canvas *and* the paint to create one's life!

The overarching implication of these visceral experiences of connectedness is that my individuality is at once a reality and an illusion. On the one hand, my individual existence is supremely powerful and can have an immense impact on the Universe. At the same time, I am a miniscule part of the Universe, which is a single, connected energy vibrating at its own supreme frequency. The creative action, then, is to always be in positive resonance with this larger frequency – the divine – for my individual existence to exercise positive meaning, value or impact. And when I am in resonance, I, even as a tiny individual, have the leverage to move mountains!

The construct of separateness and its implications became particularly relevant for me when I took my personal insights and creative explorations to larger-scale, community-based endeavors. For one, I observed how intensely 'identity' is at the heart of everything artist-and-activist. What nationality or ethnicity or sexuality or gender does someone identify with? She identifies as Muslim American, or he identifies as Italian American, or 'they' identify as transgender or as people-of-color...and so on. I grew deeply puzzled. I could understand the need for terminology that was less presumptive and more accepting and allowing for all possibilities of being. And yet, ironically, these terms were reinforcing separateness at a progressively finer grain: In an effort to create inclusivity they were causing greater mutual exclusivity!

In a particularly poignant case, a good friend frequently situated her perspective in 'identity' while chatting with me on various issues, prefacing most of her statements with, "In *my* community, we think that…" or "In *my* faith we believe that…" Every time she started her discussions with prefaces like these, I found myself jarringly separated from her, tongue-tied and momentarily unable to freely and open-heartedly relate with her, with simple humanity. In those instants, I became the 'other': the one *not* in her community, *not* part of her faith, and so on. As soon as she called out her identity in an effort to contextualize her perspective or to assert her independently recognizable existence, an invisible wall was erected between us, a wall that I had already seen crumble between the homeless man and me! Because I knew this truth, I realized that to make a heartfelt connection with my friend, I must make a conscious effort to transcend the invisible walls of safety and survival she habitually erects around herself, naming this enclosure her 'identity.'

I had long had a vague instinct about the futility of national and religious barriers, but when notions of identity began crumbling in this way for me, I clearly saw the fallacy of other, larger aggregates of identity as well, whether geographical, physical or virtual: a neighborhood, a religion, a nation, or even a planet or a solar system. Like the short-term benefits of compartmentalization within oneself, I could see the logistical and operational benefits of these separations within the larger organism that is collective human existence, but I realized how important it is to be conscious that that's all they are, functional conveniences. Every time the spiritual unity transcending these illusory divisions is forgotten, humanity suffers greatly.

Eventually, in a heart-to-heart, my friend clarified that her prefacing references helped her provide context for "where she was coming from." Although I understood this, I had experienced the limited and even divisive use of such context, so I began practicing awareness of my own use of them. I stopped asking others where they are from, or what they do, at least not as ways to genuinely get to know them. 'Indian-American' became a useless label for me, at best a convenience for others – so that they can contextualize their life experiences in contrast to mine – reinforcing duality and separateness between us.

For my part, I dropped any nationalistic or ethnic terms to describe myself. Eventually I also saw that while writing, singing, designing, painting, directing and coaching are creative things I *do*, I am *not* a writer, musician, architect, visual artist, director or coach. Neither am I a thirty-seven-year-old, woman-of-color. I am simply a being, who is simultaneously nothing and everything. At any given moment I am just one probabilistic position in a landscape of endless possibilities!

It is human to find solace in association and belonging, so perhaps it is far too vulnerable for us to relinquish these attachments! Yet, in this vulnerability, in this 'death' of separateness and identity lies the gift of truth, of connectedness, of spiritual oneness, of the divine.

Connectedness in Human Systems:
Only as Strong as Our Weakest Link

"We must recognize that the suffering of one person or one nation is the suffering of humanity. That the happiness of one person or nation is the happiness of humanity."

– The Dalai Lama

Once I experienced Universal connectedness, other insights surfaced rapidly. Many of these have to do with how groups function and move in space and time, both as a collection of individuals and as one unified being within the larger organism of universal existence. Because the last two years brought many creative endeavors that focused on building and shaping communities, I was able to practice and hone these insights.

A particular insight is that in any team – whether a couple in a relationship, hiking or dance partners, or a larger group – two things can happen, and paradoxically, they are not mutually exclusive. One is synergy in the system, so that its total potential is much greater than the sum of its parts. The other is that the system is always only as strong as its weakest link.[41] Both these phenomena are outcomes of our connectedness within and with the system.

Synergies are recognized more easily and celebrated more readily. When there is a 'weakness' in a system, however, the tendency is to use denial or brute force to push forward regardless. We refuse to do the difficult work of addressing the weak link – either lending a hand as needed, or recognizing that the system can only be so strong or so fast. Further still, we miss seeing our individual and collective connectedness with the 'weak link.' We neglect to inquire into how it is either an opportunity for growth for the entire system (not just the individual 'weak link'), or how it may be the true representation of the total potential of the system, or whether it may actually be the *right* thing for the entire system, even representing its innate strength! Instead, we resort to the 'potted plants' way of viewing the collective, isolating the 'weak link' and trying to fix it independently, or worse still, apathetically leaving it behind or even severing it.

---

41. I don't use the term 'weak' as a value judgment, but to encompass all meanings of 'less,' whether slower in pace or evolution, or lower in physical or emotional strength or awareness, etc.

Take for example, the situation of a newly forming romantic relationship. To progress healthily, the relationship must grow at a pace that respects the person who needs or wants to take it slower. The same goes for a group of people hiking up a mountain together; different people can hike at their individual paces, but all in all, the group's collective pace is going to be determined by the slowest and most deliberate hiker. In both cases, the 'slower' person is as much an asset to the entire system as they might appear to be a liability. In the case of the romantic relationship, the opportunity may be for the couple to savor the slow but steady deepening of their relationship and build a solid foundation together, a benefit to the system of their couplehood. In the case of the group of hikers, the opportunity may be for everyone to not only experience the surrounds with more richness and presence, but also to focus on building strength over cardiovascular fitness!

The corollary of this, of course, is that the collective output of a group or community is represented not just by the highest and best within the group, but also by the lowest and weakest, and in fact, sometimes, largely by the latter. Take the example of running into a frothing-at-the-mouth fundamentalist of any religious group, and how easily such an experience could color our impression of the entire religion, and its corresponding community. Or, consider how one grossly negative experience with a salesperson of a store can drastically change our overall impression of the store. As marketing guru Seth Godin wrote in a recent blog post, "The worst experience of a brand *is* the brand"!

This became apparent to me through my multiple years of experience with both participating in and directing *Yoni ki Baat* in Seattle. Each year we worked hard to source and share original stories of womanhood, sexuality and survival. As a community, some of us were intentional about remembering that a bold and unapologetic presentation of women's issues and taboo topics need not necessarily equate to attacking or stereotyping men (or for that matter, any group). In spite of our concerted efforts to create a wide range of thoughtful and groundbreaking stories, many people in the audience often remembered a particular year's program by the single story that did slip into stereotyping men or characterizing them in negative light. So, each year, no matter how spiritually or philosophically or creatively elevated any individual contribution was, we were collectively only as strong as our weakest link!

This insight made me reflect on my own role in a connected group or community. Simply disassociating from a group is the same as living the illusion that I am a separate, distinct being, while simply charging on ahead to lead a group with my own insights merely creates an illusion of progress. In the end, I found that it requires a delicate balancing act between forging my own path and remaining consciously connected to the 'pathfinders' of every collective of which I am a part.

In the context of *Yoni ki Baat*, it meant realizing that the true work of such an endeavor is to heal and transform the hurt hearts of the women participating – every single one of them without exception – with a process of love and creative exploration, and ultimately, arrive at a place in which our stories would naturally and authentically speak of courage and fortitude without slipping into bitterness or attacks on others. So long as even a single woman was left behind with her hurt unhealed and her heart unchanged, our job as a collective and as a movement was left incomplete.

Extending this thought to a larger scale it becomes evident that so long as someone in this world is poor and hungry, uneducated and isolated, battered and oppressed…our first-world existence is an illusion, because *we are they and they are us*. Our work as a human collective is incomplete; we are only as strong as our weakest link!

Connectedness Within and Without:
At War with Oneself

"There is no Them. There are only facets of Us."

– John Michael Green

A particularly endearing aspect of my interactions with Andrew held the key to a fuller comprehension of connectedness within and without, and its larger implications. Though I have experienced this to some degree in other relationships and friendships, it is almost without exception that when Andrew and I 'argue' about anything, it is like having an energetic, passionate, caring internal discourse with myself. It is just as though I were exploring and fleshing out the different ways of looking at an issue or subject within my own self, except that I am doing this with him. In other words, when we debate and argue and even downright disagree about something, *he is I and I am he*. And no matter how much

I might disagree in the moment with whatever he is saying, his words and perspective always seep into my heart as an aspect of the truth that will become relevant in some imminent situation or context. So, what I experience is that even in conflict, he and I are on the same side: on *our* side.

How fundamentally would all conflict (and relationships) transform with this simple switch toggled on, the realization that two people can always remain connected and on the same side, especially in conflict? Why must conflict necessarily be oppositional, even when it is a tension of opposing forces or ideas or needs? Conflict is necessary for growth, for revealing our unhealed aspects, to nurture and heal them once brought forth, and finally, transform them into opportunities for new, positive creation. But such healing and creation can only happen when two (or more) people can remember even in the throes of deep conflict that they are, ultimately, on the same side. Moving in parallel and coming from a place of inquiry and exploration have made Andrew's and my conversations (and arguments!) deeply clarifying, broadening, enriching and delightful.

When we become separated in conflict – in 'us versus them' – we are, in truth, at war with ourselves. In one of my ongoing visions of being connected seamlessly to everyone around me, I saw the entire world as one contiguous living and breathing organism, analogous to my own contiguous physical body. So, it occurred to me that America being at war with Iraq or Afghanistan is like my hand attacking, say, my own little toe!

When does one part of a body attack another? Unconsciously, it does so in an auto-immune condition, such as AIDS or Multiple Sclerosis, that is, in states of physical disease. Consciously, it might do so in other diseased conditions like cancer, when intentionally severing a body part due to its proliferating without control is necessary, because its behavior is detrimental to the health and well-being of the overall body system. In spite of relief, however, the body knows that it just amputated a part of itself. It is not under the illusion that it was 'them' – the enemy – that it defeated; it knows well that it sacrificed one aspect of itself for holistic good, and it does its share of acknowledging and grieving this loss, while celebrating its renewed ability to heal and thrive.

Needless to say, going to war is a conscious choice. So, how would things be different if, every time we thought we needed to go to war with another faction, tribe or nation, all our considerations were similar in intention and sincerity to those made before we choose to sever a part of our own body in a cancerous state? How would the energy and focus shift, and how might our choices be different? At the very least, how would the story we tell ourselves and the world about going to war, change?

Like being on the same side as an arguing couple in a relationship, all of a sudden, we would see that ultimately, as a team or a country, we are really on the same side as the very 'enemy' whom we are going to combat: on the side of *our* world, our universal cosmic existence as a whole. It then behooves each of us individually and collectively at the level of global consciousness, to reflect, be and act as one organism – living, breathing, loving – our combined existence. Then and only then will we be doing the right thing and acting out of love, at every turn and in every moment. And I wonder how often we would go to war at all if we saw with such unfettered clarity that all war is, in truth, war with oneself.

Connected Healing and Transformation:
The Power of Collective Creativity

"By sharing our stories, we can see our connectedness and catalyze change in the broader social fabric shaping our lives."

– Nan Bauer Maglin

In the chapter Creativity, I talked about arriving at the realization that creativity is not only our innate divine gift, but that exercising it in this world is our true life purpose, that we are here to create our reality, and that we do it anyway, either consciously or unconsciously. While creativity is powerful at the individual level, once I became viscerally aware of my spiritual connectedness with other beings, I began seeing the immense power of 'collective creativity,' the conscious and intentional exercise of creative power in larger groups.

Most people can feel the palpable energy in a large room full of people doing Yoga together, or in a place of worship with people praying together. Following my Vipassana meditation experience, I became acutely sensitive to and in tune with the collective energy in the room in various situations, whether positive or negative. So, I began reflecting on the idea that along with private and personal exercises in healing and transformation through therapy, meditation and creative ventures, there could be an immense, exponentially magnified power in collective exercises of the same. Of course, the idea of group therapy and healing is nothing new; it is rather commonly used in addressing issues of survival, recovery from substance abuse, etc. I became interested, however, in the possibilities of translating shared experience and stories into collective *creative* product.

As I've mentioned before, in 2010 two projects came my way in quick succession. One was the 'zine *Courageous Creativity*, in which my partner Shirin and I began curating and publishing personal stories of courage, creativity and change. The other was Seattle's 2011 *Yoni ki Baat*, which I was invited to direct. In doing both projects, phenomenal things happened, not only for me and the other participants at the individual level, but also for the group and people in their spheres of influence, at the collective level.

The first thing I noticed about projects involving collective creativity is the lightning speed with which they gain momentum, especially when conceived in love and highest intentions. Nearly effortlessly, people and resources materialize from nowhere, exactly how and when one needs them. In curating and editing *Courageous Creativity*, every month Shirin and I wondered: Can we really put up yet another rich, thoughtful issue? Over the course of a few issues, we saw that all we had to do is envision it, believe in it, and then, of course, do the (rigorous but easy!) work of spotting connections with our chosen theme for the month, and lo and behold! Somehow, each month, we had another brilliant issue with diverse contributors and rich, meaningful stories. And with each round, our readership and list of potential contributors grew too.

I believe that all this happened because *Courageous Creativity* taps collective creativity at two levels. One is at the level of the visionary team – of Shirin and I – whose loving friendship, resonance and combined purpose are being harnessed into meaningful action, and adding to that mix, Sam, our graphic designer, who has similarly resonant values. The other level is the collective of diverse contributors in each issue, who might otherwise be strangers to each other, but who become powerfully connected by virtue of storytelling within a shared theme and purpose. At both these levels, collective creative power is harnessed, and is putting into motion the next level of creative iteration for the 'zine.

The next impact of collective creativity that I've observed is a heightened level of transparency, authenticity and integrity in the lives of all those who participate in these projects, whether as contributors or as audience members. As my massage therapist and

Reiki healer David once said to me, "We are only as sick as our secrets." Writing or story-telling with collective commitment to transparency and integrity, such as in *Yoni ki Baat*, means that we no longer hide in shame or blame. We take responsibility for our stories and speak our truths, with love. And we do so in an audience's witness, who also take responsibility by listening, holding, and receiving these stories. The outcome of this connected collaboration is phenomenal. Large collectives shed baggage, walk with a lighter step, hold their heads high, and become more welcoming, receiving, loving, and creative.

Along with this, participants experience an intense transformation in their personal lives as well. Through the collective storytelling in both *Courageous Creativity* and in *Yoni ki Baat*, every individual reports being substantially transformed in fundamental ways that spark immediate, recognizable and quantum shifts in their current lives. Things become unstuck, and previously inaccessible avenues begin to manifest. Some new opportunity might open up, a past issue might inexplicably resolve itself, broken or failing relationships might mend, negative influences might disappear, health or finances might improve, and so on. Nothing short of miracles occurs, and people start becoming aware of their power to (re)create their own lives.

The final outcome from all this is often a resonant buzz in the larger community, not simply of 'news,' but of inspiration and action. Suddenly, other writers, magazines, storytelling ventures and such begin to appear and grow. It is as if one plants the seed for a movement, and soon, one isn't even the founder or author of that movement – it has an organic, creative life of its own – it now procreates and multiplies in significance and relevance using its own innate power. It has, as the marketing folks like to say, viral power!

In a relatively unknown sociological experiment, in the summer of 1993, four thousand people practiced transcendental meditation in Washington D.C. with an intention to lower crime in the area, and succeeding in doing so by twenty-three percent! (Rigorous statistical analyses ruled out alternative explanations, and the odds of such results by chance are less than two in one billion.) This story makes me wonder what degree of impact we could collectively have on our communities, other parts of the world, or the Universe by committing to always carrying positive energy together, connecting the dots in our stories, and creating new possibilities together. Collective creativity can change the entire courses of communities, countries, the planet, and the entire Universe!

I am all, all are me

Connectedness is the awareness that because we are each a connected part of a bigger whole, what is outside myself is a reflection of what is inside myself, and vice-versa. It is the knowing that every good and every evil is at once out there and in here, and that each action really does have a corresponding reaction somewhere in our connected, collective existence.

Connectedness in action is:

– Living an integrated existence within, of a continuous, connected field of luscious green (instead of compartmentalized 'potted plants'), by connecting with my whole energetic existence;

– Transcending any attachments with association, belonging and identity to allow a 'death' of separateness – the notion of myself as a separate being – and to find the authentic power in spiritual oneness with others;

– Recognizing that the connected system of all beings can only be as strong or fast or healed as the weakest link, and acknowledging my personal responsibility towards this collective effort;

– Remaining on the same side with others, especially in conflict, knowing that all war is ultimately, war with myself;

– Leveraging the immense power of collective creativity, enabling heightened levels of transparency, authenticity, integrity and transformation in the lives of entire communities.

In moments of experiencing connectedness, I can see that every vibration, every breath, and every event in my individual existence is part of a much, much bigger flow. Thriving is about remaining connected and in positive resonance with this overarching frequency, so that my individual existence can create meaning, value and positive evolution for all beings.

For Shirin

7.
COMMITMENT

Commitment is the unfailing faith in one's Higher Power, and the act of wholeheartedly and unequivocally choosing love and life every single day.

I choose my life – every day!

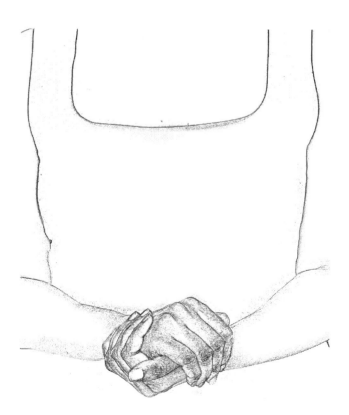

Committing to Faith:
Believe and You Shall See

"Commitment unlocks the doors of imagination, allows vision, and gives us the "right stuff" to turn our dreams into reality."

– James Womack

With a few years of practice in centering, consciousness, compassion, choice and creativity, and then, opening up to connectedness within myself and with the world, I stumbled upon … well, commitment.[42] If this ubiquitous and over-used word in personal and professional terms seems like either an anti-climax or a no-brainer in the series of chapters in this book, let me confess that for me, it showed up as quite the surprise. The challenge of commitment – the depths in which it revealed itself to me – came hurtling around a blind corner, so I was really taken aback! Yes, on most days I am accessing my Higher Power and creating my life with love. But what about the times I am not, the times in which fear, doubt, anxiety and resistance rear their ugly heads, and threaten to take over and consume me? What am I to do in *those* times?

In such times, the only way I know how to come out of the hole is to become completely still using my Vipassana meditation skills, and listen patiently above the deafening noise, without becoming critical of myself. What I can do quite rapidly then, is to tell the surface storms of the sea apart from the quietness, stillness, depth, stability and calm of the majestic ocean. I can recognize that I am the ocean, and not its surface storms. My Higher Power whispers: "Start over, Shahana. Locate your center. Access your consciousness. Source compassion. Exercise choice and creativity. Stay connected. And commit to doing this all over again today, because today is a brand new day!"[43]

---

42. In my original outline for *Thrive!*, which has barely changed through the two years of writing, this final chapter was titled Continuity, meant to elaborate on the continuous practice of all the other six Cs. But in the course of writing and editing this book, Shirin and I realized that continuity of practice is really about commitment!

43. It is important to see these times not as "regressions," but rather as times of forgetting or disconnecting from one's Higher Power, which is always already available, only moments away from being remembered. Once remembered, it is instantly accessible and there is a quantum leap into one's creative power; it is not much of a 'process' all over again. If it ever feels like a laborious process, it's a good sign that one is stuck on a treadmill, and not really connected to one's Higher Power.

And what is the strength behind this daily commitment? Always, it is love and faith. It is the faith I have in the hand hovering over my head in blessing, of which I had a vision, back in 2005. It is the faith I have in the limitless skies, deepest of waters, and tiniest of wild, yellow flowers glistening on a mossy rock in a ray of sunshine that sneaked through the trees. It is the faith I have in myself, and in my Higher Power. Love and faith compel me to take that next step, to start over, again and again, even when I do not see how or when it will all work out. I see that, in truth, it all does *always* works out!

We're conditioned into the idea that "seeing is believing": Only that which can be seen is 'real.' Once I came into my consciousness and my creativity, I knew that believing actually precedes seeing; that is, whatever we can imagine and believe in, we can manifest into reality. Whether it is the vision I have for the world, the kind of work I want to do, the health or prosperity I wish to achieve, or the kind of relationships I desire in my life, *anything* is possible! I have to first imagine it with love, then believe in it consistently with inspiration and grace, and then take the actions that naturally reveal themselves. I have to commit to unwavering faith. I have to commit to believing in belief itself!

In the earlier stages of practice in commitment, the irony is that the more I commit to my faith, the more fear, doubt, anxiety, guilt and resistance rear their ugly heads, sometimes every single day. It is as if the negative force knows to swell and rise in direct proportion to the magnitude of my faith and love. The only way is to keep being present to not only the feelings of fear within my own mind, but also many an 'external' circumstance or incident or person, which come by freely, invited in by my own fear to attempt to topple my faith!

If one is looking for these in one's life, I've discovered that they present themselves as random events, but they are not really! They may appear, say, on the day of an important interview, in the form of a sudden headache, or a missed bus due to an error in the schedule, or an untimely argument picked by someone else, or an unexpected traffic jam, or a weather switcheroo…in each case, it is simply a failure of one's inner faith. This is why I pause to check myself every time I tell other people of such 'reasons' for not doing something, or being late to something. At these times, I smile with recognition of my fear in action, and invite love to take over. And if I'm still not going to do something, the most truthful statement would be, "I choose and commit to something else right now." This is because, having experienced complete connectedness, I know that every external event, whether an obstacle or an enabler, is the reflection of either the voice of fear or the force of love within me!

Often fear, doubt and anxiety are expressed through *other* people in one's life, who feel these things on one's behalf, ostensibly out of 'love' or 'concern': a paranoid parent who worries excessively, a managing spouse who caretakes, an over-protective friend who cautions against the dark forces out there, the insurance agent who portends disasters in one's life, the doctor who insists on medicating a cold with an antibiotic…again, each case is simply a reflection of what is within, because within and without are entirely connected. When such people or voices show up in my life, I express gratitude for their valuable presence in my life to show me the truth of my inner state. Then I become present to those inner fears that they're reflecting, and then, by inviting love, I consciously choose to create the outcome that is highest and best for me.

Recently I was in a freak accident, which exemplifies some of the aforementioned phenomena. Carrying a heavy suitcase up the stairs to my friend Bipasha's apartment, where I was temporarily staying in-between house moves, I lost my balance and clipped the entire big-toenail off my left foot with my right heel. This was the night before I was scheduled to fly to Los Angeles for a consulting assignment. My toe gushed blood non-stop as I held it under the faucet in the bathtub, and standing there on one leg in a red pool, I became overcome with panic. My anxiety was not only about my toe, but suddenly about everything: leaving town, moving back into my condo right after I returned, my upcoming financial and other responsibilities, and so on. Later, I sobbed on the bed with excruciating pain, attempting to elevate my foot and ice it to stop the bleeding.

When Bipasha returned home, she was, of course, immediately concerned. Taking one look at my injured toe, she urged that we rush to the hospital. By this time though, I was beginning to center myself, replacing the chaos of fear with the calm of love. While Bipasha, rightly from her point of view, couldn't imagine how I'd fly the next day in such a condition, worrying that I would cause a terrible infection if I didn't get medical attention right away and so on, I had already begun to internally invoke my body's innate ability to heal itself. I thanked her, and let her know that I wanted to allow my body to heal itself. Although she was initially disturbed at what probably appeared as stubbornness or avoidance on my part, she eventually acquiesced to the route I was choosing, and decided to do some Internet research about self-care in my condition. We uncovered all the necessary steps for proper healing, and she generously went to the drugstore to arm me with supplies of Hydrogen Peroxide, Epsom salt, anti-bacterial cream, gauze and bandaids.

The next morning Bipasha was still fearful for me, and thought that she spotted the telltale bluishness and radiating streaks of red on my foot that the Web site had warned of, in cases of infection. I thanked her again for her concern and all her help, but remained firmly rooted in my faith. Although I traveled to Los Angeles with a really painful and swollen foot, I continued to lovingly channel my body's healing powers throughout my flight. I was immensely grateful for all the help and caring Bipasha had given me, and sent love her way as well.

Then I brought consciousness to all my own fears, realizing that they had manifested not only Bipasha's fears for me, but also the freak accident in the first place. I saw that the entire incident was a reflection of my resisting my current life situation. So I chose it all fully: the unexpected consulting trip, the upcoming move, and the financial responsibilities. Within only two days of nursing my toe in the Los Angeles hotel room, it began making miraculous strides in healing. I was at peace to do my work with complete choice and commitment, and all my worries melted away. My faith turned everything around and manifested anew: physical healing, an enjoyable and inspiring work experience, and a safe return to Seattle to take on my upcoming responsibilities.

Again and again I see that it is pointless to fight the fear; the only way is to give it my listening and compassion, knowing that it is here to loyally protect my little self, my ego. The way forward is to simply be still and love more. And to commit, again and again, to faith, to joy, to love, to my Higher Power, and to life itself.

Committing to Living:
Life is a Verb!

"You have a choice. Live or die. Every breath is a choice. Every minute is a choice. To be or not to be."

– Chuck Palahniuk

The principal insight that I gained about commitment through my daily practice of creativity is that, instead of the future-oriented way in which commitment is traditionally understood, it is entirely a present-oriented effort. Commitment has come to be represented by things such as the one-year consulting agreement, the two-year cell phone contract, the fifteen-year mortgage, and the lifelong marriage. Such a representation of commitment perpetuates the notion that it is housed in that one-time external effort – the signing up for something – after which one basically has to fulfill its requirements. This is a passive, uncreative stance. In the active stance – as an act of creation – commitment is *starting over every single moment*, choosing love and choosing life each time, wholeheartedly and unequivocally. Commitment is about doing the highest and best in this moment and in this moment alone...again and again.

Now, you might wonder, doesn't everybody choose love and life over other alternatives? Well, most of us don't actually. Some consciously choose fear and death, and many of us unconsciously choose to gradually whittle and wither away, paralyzed by the idea that we might actually live up to our singular potential, while outwardly amassing false markers of 'success' and 'prosperity.' We become content with fulfilling various contractual requirements, believing that this makes us 'committed,' and we refuse to do the real work of committing, to creating our own lives. The human condition is that because we're afraid of death, quite paradoxically, we respond by acting as if we have all the time in the world to waste away!

Patti Digh's profoundly moving book *Life is a Verb: 37 Days to Wake Up, Be Mindful, and Live Intentionally*, was conceived from her award-winning blog *37Days*. This blog was born out of her experience of witnessing her stepfather die a mere thirty-seven days after being diagnosed with lung cancer. In the blog Patti writes, *"What emerged was a renewed commitment to ask myself this question every morning: What would I be doing today if I only had 37 days to live?"* Patti's answer to this question gave rise not only to her blog, but also three books and countless inspirational talks through which she has shared her insights with thousands, and changed many lives. But more importantly, her answer fundamentally changed her view of what it means to be a human being on a daily basis, as a wife, mother, and citizen of the world. She committed to only the present moment, in every role and every context, every moment of her life.

I learned to make life a verb on a daily basis through my practice of creativity. In the chapter Creativity, I described how in late 2008, I had stepped away from a corporate career to spend a few months with my core gifts: writing, painting, and singing. Before I knew it, daily creativity became a habit that lasted a full year...then two, and beyond! The effortful, joyous, daily action – through craft, through body, through insight, through service

– fundamentally changed my way of being. In the advance practice of my creativity, I began having the experience of simply being a channel through which the divine was creating, and so, I understood that the divine-I, as one unified being, was creating life itself. The expression 'leading a life,' which I used to read in conjunction with wise sages and seers in old Indian mythology, suddenly became poignant: *I am the leader of my life*, which means I choose it, I create it and I thrive in it. And every one of these – *choose, create, thrive* – is a verb, a definite, unequivocal commitment to action, every day!

So, first and foremost, commitment means taking total personal responsibility. There is little room for blaming others, circumstances past or present, the economy, government, war, or gravity. Commitment means fully owning and exercising my choice and creative power for determining my life course.

Next, commitment leaves no room for equivocation. There is little place for 'maybe,' 'perhaps,' 'someday,' 'sort of,' 'kind of,' and the like. It is telling that most people's everyday language is fraught with these terms of prevarication. Speaking in clear, straight, committed terms is frightening for most of us, because it means we would have to actually *be* who we say we are! So instead, we safely paint an apologetic, half-hearted picture of ourselves, hiding behind the sham of 'humility.' In his call-to-action book *Do the Work*, Steven Pressfield says – unequivocally – that if your feelings are anywhere but on the far right of the spectrum '*Dabbling • Interested • Intrigued but Uncertain • Passionate • Totally Committed*,' don't even bother doing the work!

And finally, commitment requires uncompromised discipline. It asks that every morning start with love and joy. It demands that on those mornings when resistance and fear groan and protest in cacophony, I must consciously access my Higher Power, and choose life. This choice is not just a thought or a mantra; it really is an action. It translates to jumping out of bed, meeting my day with presence, gratitude and enthusiasm, and turning to the discipline of doing the creative work, whatever that might be on that day.

COMMITMENT

Committing to Dying:
Closing Doors to Open Doors

"…And so long as you haven't experienced this: to die and so to grow,
you are only a troubled guest on the dark earth."

– Johann Wolfgang von Goethe, *The Holy Longing*

Because commitment demands that we choose everything we do fully and un-equivocally, its corollary, in an apparently opposite action, is to consciously and intention-ally shed, edit, and prune everything that does *not* fit with what we've committed to. After all, if one keeps all options open at all times, that is really just another way of never com-mitting to anything!

Our culture emphasizes having options. Of course we like having options in our material consumption, researching on end to find the 'right' product, but we bring this obsession with options to every aspect of our lives. We interview in multiple places so that we have options for a place of employment; we interview several candidates for an open position. We meet different people for an ideal romantic partner; we scan various others for the best business partner. And we nurture various, sometimes mundane social relationships just in case we're excluded from the in-crowd. We are advised not to burn bridges, not to close doors.

So, there's an ingrained tendency to keep various doors open, even though one is presumably focused on a particular, well-chosen path. Especially as an artist-entrepreneur, it might seem like an appropriate and sensible measure: Should this idea or initiative not take off, surely I should have another one in hand from my wellspring of ideas, ready to test and launch? Isn't that what entrepreneurship, creativity and innovation are about: trying out idea after idea, and always having lots of ideas available?

More often than not, however, open doors cause leaks. Just like air leaks out of a house if a door is open, energy leaks out of a creative initiative and depletes its resources if a door is left open. It is almost as if one is ever so slightly, imperceptibly, insidiously distracted, disabling that fully enthusiastic, unequivocal, dedicated and all-consuming energetic commitment that imbues an initiative with a wholehearted chance at success.

Languishing in the company of a romantic ex-partner, for example, could have the effect of a leaky door. It could leak emotional energy, compromising the forming or deepening of a new relationship. Similarly, in the name of 'staying in touch,' spending too much energy keeping abreast of the ongoings or changes in an old employer's enterprise could compromise truly new career opportunities from arising or maturing. And as an artist-entrepreneur, remaining attached to a previous innovation or idea can prevent new ones from getting their full, uncompromised energy and focus.

Why, then, do we keep doors open? Yes, it is the work of the usual suspect – fear – that faithful old friend of survival. We fear loss, missed opportunity, the unfamiliar, the free-fall. And we fear that closing doors will limit or close-off our options, lock us in a dead-end, make us claustrophobic. This is nothing but a fear of commitment itself!

In 2010 I discovered that taking the chance to fully close doors can almost immediately open new doors, quickly, efficiently, energetically and creatively. Because I had completely closed the door to an old employer, new opportunities that I simply could not have envisioned within that old framework, began to emerge. Because I finally had the courage to completely abandon a creative business idea (that is, accept failure at it), the idea for a brand new one was able to take off with uncanny momentum. Ending some relationships – in some cases dysfunctional and in others harmless but divergent in purpose – began opening the doors to new, thriving, creatively directional ones. Jason and I ended our romantic relationship of three years with mutual respect, understanding and caring. Closing the door to this relationship romantically released locked up energy for much creative use.

Frequently, the closed door opens a new door to the same employer, the same business idea, the same relationship! For instance, I was able to consult on multiple exciting projects with the Los Angeles office of my old firm, and have great fun as well as mutual fulfillment in doing so. Equally happily, Jason and I found ourselves able to begin a more meaningful and supportive friendship than we'd been able to achieve as romantic partners. In these new openings, the debate is reframed, the entire premise is new, and so the opportunity and course are new too.

With greater and greater authenticity in my life, relationships, situations and projects fell away naturally as they became poor fits, unserving of my spiritual and creative evolution. I had to learn to allow this to happen, and eventually, even initiate it. At first I practiced recognizing the instances in which organic shedding was occurring, and experiencing them like the Fall season, when trees naturally shed all their leaves, and start over. I learned to cultivate a level of detachment and allow the shedding to occur even as I experienced some sadness. Next, I learned to become my own gardener and sculptor. Instead of waiting for the shedding to happen by default, I learned to consciously and intentionally prune at the right times. This meant cultivating the ability to recognize, listen, and then act on my Higher Power's message, "Shahana, this thing is done. Let go (with love), and move forward."

Mustering the courage to tightly but lovingly close doors – without vacillation or equivocation – is an essential aspect of commitment. And I find that it always holds a surprise on the other end! Instead of claustrophobia, I experience unexpected, expansive openings of opportunity and creative energy. Every healthy tree needs pruning to keep growing stronger, richer, and deeper! By committing to being a healthy, evolving, thriving tree, pruning out everything that is inauthentic to me in the present – activities, relationships, constructs of self, the past, stories about myself, and so on – I've also committed to *dying before I die*, as Eckhart Tolle puts it in *The Power of Now*, so that I can be reborn every day! When such a death is died every single day, one is thriving.

Extending this insight, a thriving life is ultimately an active, conscious preparation for a beautiful, honest, and enlightened passing – into the next realm. No matter what one believes about what happens after physical death, thriving is about welcoming that transitional moment in one's highest consciousness – choosing and creating the experience of passing from one form to another – and the journey of the soul thereafter. Instead of death randomly knocking on my door by circumstantial events or by my body's unconscious failure, commitment to dying daily to the past allows me to have conscious, creative choice in the matter of my physical death. My passing into the other realm can then occur as part of the practice of centering, compassion, consciousness, choice, creativity and connectedness in this life! At the helm of such practice, there opens the possibility for 'icchha mrtiyu,' roughly translated from Sanskrit as 'death by design,' which was available to great souls like The Buddha, Jesus, and Bhishma in The Mahabharata.

Committing to Myself:
What's My Story?

"I think it's your own choice if you turn from an angry young man to a bitter, old bastard."

– Bille Joe Armstrong

In choosing life daily and making it an active verb, a significant aspect of commitment that revealed itself to me is the story I choose to tell about myself. Throughout this book I've discussed past and future, self-concept and identity, all of which needed to break down and dissolve, for me to lead a thriving life. Still, every word we say about ourselves, to others or in our own heads, remains ridden with continuously forming conceptions about the self. A simple friendly inquiry by someone getting to know me, such as, "So, what do you do?" brings forth all the complexities of identity tied to 'work.' What do I choose to say in these moments? That I am a design strategist? That I am an architect, artist, musician, and writer? Or that I am a creativity catalyst and teacher? Or that really, I am nothing but a perennial student? What's my story?

Although work is culturally so connected to self-concept, relationships are powerful mirrors to reveal much about it as well. One of my most delightful insights came in my relationship with Jason, with whom I was ridiculously and hilariously incompatible in my need for deep conversation. Jason habitually gave me monosyllabic answers when I inquired about his day, however remarkable it might have been. Typically, he followed this by the quid-pro-quo, asking me about my day, and then promptly turning on the television on high volume, to flick channels as I talked. This, of course, drove me insane, and over time I was forced to devise a coping mechanism.

I began to tell Jason about my day in fewer than two sentences, no matter how richly complex or eventful it had been. It was the only way I had any luck gaining either his attention or his recall. Although the channel-flicking didn't help the emotional richness and intimacy required to have a meaningful relationship, in spite of my frustration (and at times, grave annoyance), I learned something personally important. I discovered that while it was deeply fulfilling to relate my day's story to a like-spirited friend interested in the nuances and rich complexities of my experiences, talking with Jason was often liberating, and even illuminating in other ways!

By reducing my story to its most distilled form, I found myself relinquishing the charge or drama related to the day's events. I became more factual and objective, making it less personal, less 'about me.' In a two-sentence story, a "disastrous argument with an irate colleague that exploded into a two-hour scene," might turn into, "a disagreement that took a couple of hours to resolve." Or, "my excruciating migraine that only released after the chiropractor put my habitually twisting out atlas back in place," might become, "a migraine that came and went." The distilled accounts offered me an alternative way of looking at the same story, with a valuable simplicity and an empowering detachment.

So, although I had already begun speaking my truths with greater vulnerability and authenticity, free of concepts of identity and self-concept, I now became increasingly aware that the particular truths – the *specific* story – I choose to tell about myself holds massive creative power. Storytelling is a form of committing to the way I desire to be, thereby putting that desire into creation through every word spoken in every moment! We mistakenly believe that the stories we tell can only be those of the past, that which has already happened. When we are committed to storytelling only of the present, a powerful creative force is unleashed, birthing the immediate future, that which is yet to happen.

My friend and partner Shirin had a profound experience of this phenomenon. In the wake of leaving her longtime job and starting the publishing venture with me, she often told people who asked her what she did for a living, the longer story, the story rooted in the past, founded in explanation. "I worked for an insurance company as a software engineer for thirteen years, but after my second son was born, I thought I should be more available as a mother…and I thought I could also pursue my interest in writing and other community activities on the side…," and so forth. Then suddenly one day when someone asked her the same question at a party, she heard herself saying, "I am the co-founder of a publishing platform and its online 'zine called *Courageous Creativity.*" With this simpler, shorter, but most importantly, more *present* story, Shirin found herself standing taller, with passion and joy coursing through her veins. In that moment she was alive: She was thriving! And in the months that followed, Shirin was able to inject fresh energy and leadership into *Courageous Creativity*, making it ascend to the next level of quality, impact and audience response!

So, yes, I had an emotionally and physically violent childhood and marriage. Yes, I spent most of my twenties in desperation and suffering. Yes, I developed significant physical ailments over time, including excruciating migraines, gut problems, hair loss and immune reactions like food allergies. Yet, all this is, as authors Chip and Dan Heath have referenced it in their latest book *Switch*, TBU: True But Useless! Or what Jack Canfield, author of *Chicken Soup for the Soul*, calls the "So-what?" of my life!

In *Do the Work* Steven Pressfield says that to create meaningful work, things such as a sense of entitlement, impatience, fear, hope, or ego must be left behind. Additionally, all grievances and sense of personal exceptionalness associated with one's life circumstances, must also be relinquished. "*The only items you get to keep are love for the work, will to finish, and passion to serve the ethical, creative Muse,*" Pressfield writes.

The past had a significant role in making me what I am today; as I said in the opening of this book, it was the compost, the fodder, from which could bloom a thriving life. But the *narrative* of the past – the old story – has no continued use. The past was useful only because I chose to transcend it – not by rejecting, disowning or even bypassing it, but by feeling and accepting it wholeheartedly, and by using it for awakening and consciousness. Now there is a blank canvas, on which to create whatever story I choose to paint. And it is mine and mine alone to paint, every single day!

So, from here on, I commit to only the story that matters, the essential and present story. I am a creativity catalyst, teacher, and student. And I am a being in love...with the divine, with humanity and its creative potential, with life, with my friends and family, with a particular man, and with myself. Right here, right now, that's my (only) story.

Commitment is Only Within:
I Do!

"*If you deny yourself commitment, what can you do with your life?*"

– Harvey Fierstein

The 2010-2011 period had been the most creative time of my life: I had written my first book, launched a publishing platform and a powerful magazine, completed a house remodel for my ex-boyfriend Jason, held a private recital with seven of my classical music students performing, begun consulting again in design strategy, directed *Yoni ki Baat*, created an art collection ready to exhibit, resumed working on *Thrive!*, and begun coaching Creative Voice workshops…it was mind-boggling to consider it all at once! It had been an incredible two years; I had begun to fully experience what it means to leverage my Higher Power, and channel the Muse, in the service of others. I was so grateful!

In March 2011, when *Yoni ki Baat* was opened by Mimi Gardner Gates and shown to a thousand people over three sold-out nights at the Seattle Asian Art Museum, it suddenly occured to me that it was the most important work of my life thus far. Through the experience of coaching and catalyzing the courage and creativity of a diverse group of women, I was unexpectedly catapulted to a place of higher and deeper authenticity myself. Somehow I didn't see it coming, although it would seem obvious in retrospect that coaching others to bring forth their most powerful and deeply personal truths would cause me to come fully face-to-face with mine, too!

Seven years after that first experience of seeing my soul in the mirror in Andrew, we were spending time together again. With so much having evolved in between, including a three-year hiatus in physical contact, I didn't hold any expectations or preconceptions about what spending time with him would be like. As artist-entrepreneurs using our resources wisely, we ate together at humble, hole-in-the-wall restaurants in Seattle's University District. Sometimes, as special treats, we returned to an old favorite, a nicer restaurant, and occasionally, I cooked an Indian meal for us, also like old times. We sat talking and exchanging stories, creative ideas and energy in all these places – sometimes animatedly, sometimes reflectively, sometimes silently – as oblivious as ever to everything going on around us, and to the passage of time.

And I was hit with it again: *wham!* Yes, *this* is the person whose soul mirrors mine, word for word, breath for breath, idea for idea, inspiration for inspiration! You'd think I knew all this already, this uncanny, miraculous, telepathic mirroring that had shaped so much of my course since 2004. Well, of course I did, but its impact had become so integrated with my sense of being and purpose, that I had somewhat forgotten the power of the realtime soul mirroring experience. So, it was still a surprise, like a brand new, inspired realization of divine intervention, all over again.

Perhaps it was surprising because so much had happened in the last seven years, so much growth and change for the both of us. Perhaps it was surprising because the resonance was still so fresh, so genuine, so easy, so timeless, so familiar. Perhaps the mysterious and singular way in which we could telepathically intuit and understand each other, still caught me off-guard. Or perhaps it was surprising how naturally Andrew folded into my other friendships and community, any time my worlds intermingled. Anyway, here I was, facing my truth all over again. The mirror that had awakened me to my Higher Power was here again, reconnecting me with my creative potential, compelling me to re-examine the authenticity of my chosen path, and perhaps, gently egging me on to embark on the next evolution of purpose and practice. It was startling. It was moving. It was *so* loving. In my private moments of reflection, tears welled up frequently...tears of realization and gratitude, of wonderment and awe, and of deep, deep delight.

Then the external voices began to question me. They came as friends and family: "What does this mean?" "Are you guys together?" "How often do you see each other?" By now I knew, of course, that these external voices are simply signs guiding me towards inner clarity. For a while, the voices grew louder outside, and sometimes, inside. Then, just as awe-inspiring as the cosmic resonance between Andrew and I, was my Higher Power's firm prevalence over all the noise, channeled through the moments in which I remained still. She helped me answer the questions with a calm clarity: "I love Andrew at the level of soul. This love has connected me to the divine, compelled me to keep exploring my highest potential, and to help others do the same. It has inspired me to fully and unequivocally choose life. So, he is *already* my life partner!"

And then I saw it, after I had said it. Like everything else, commitment isn't what I can find outside myself, from another person, in any context, personal or professional. Commitment is only what I find inside, within me, in my own center, in my Higher Power. In the chapter Connectedness, I described how in mid-2010, several of my projects and initiatives, all poised to take off, were repeatedly getting stuck in limbo. It wasn't until I had made a shift within, and committed fully and unequivocally to select projects no matter what the outcome (while pruning out others), that they had finally taken off with Godspeed! And in the chapter Choice, I described the ultimate in choice – choosing what I have – leaning into the truth of the moment, which catapults me beyond acceptance and into commitment.

These insights now came together with perfect clarity and timing. I saw that what Andrew is going to do or not going to do with regard to 'us,' is not my concern. It only matters what *I* am going to do with regard to 'us.' I could go down the futile path of wondering or querying him about what he'd like to do, or I could simply query *myself*. I could hold still and listen, and gain inner clarity on what *I* care about, and what *I* commit to.

A little detour here has poignant bearing. When I filed for divorce back in 2005, Washington State law did not require me to provide any reasons for ending the marriage. As a no-fault-state, its stipulation for divorce is: "If one person says the marriage is over, then it is over." How terribly and shockingly simple a truth! A marriage is the union of two people. If one of the two people isn't in it, then of course there's no marriage to begin with!

Now I saw the paradoxical complement to this position: It *also* only takes one person to truly commit, in order to create a relationship! I'm not suggesting that one person can give practical, physical form to the relationship; that is created by two-way collaboration, by the unique synergy of both people involved. What I am saying, however, is that a loving, wholehearted and unequivocal commitment from one person is powerful enough (and sufficient) to create the foundation for a lasting and purposeful relationship, whatever its expressed form may be. Like love, its partner commitment, I realized, is a gift I must give freely, free of obligations, stipulations, or expectations of return. And I must do this not only for people and relationships, but also for my art, my creative projects and initiatives, and my entrepreneurial, social and humanistic endeavors. I love and commit first, and *then* the rest follows.

I reflected long and hard on this insight, for nearly nine months. I sat still, I listened for more. In doing so, my own commitment fears from all my life passed swiftly before my eyes. I saw that while I had stuck it out through thick and thin in other relationships, I had picked some inherent incompatibility to begin with. And 'making it work' in incompatible situations is a pretty ingenious way of not committing at all! Humbled by this insight, I sat still longer. Through the months of gentle stillness and a heightened practice of creativity, I heard my Higher Power consistently rise above the mental noise. "Commit!" she said. "Commit first and foremost to yourself, by submitting fully to your truth in this moment: your unconditional love for Andrew. Then commit to everything this love of yours inspires you to do: to be creative, to be a catalyst and mentor for others' creativity, to keep deep faith in mystery, magic and miracles, and to live your life with joy and awe and inspiration and love. Commit to life itself!"

And so, I did. I celebrated having love in my life – love in its ultimate avatar – as an unconditional, resonant, healing, generative and creative force. I said "I do" privately in my heart to Andrew, and then released it into the Universe. I said "I do" to all the friendships and relationships in my life that matter, determining to choose them fully, to deem them important enough to either build or prune, always with love and authenticity. I said "I do" to all my chosen creative endeavors in writing, visual art, music, design strategy, theater, creativity coaching, and building communities around shared creative purpose. And with unending gratitude I said "I do" to the divine, to Her love, grace and guidance. Most of all, I said "I do" to life itself, to honoring this incredible gift given to me. And, I committed to thriving – a continuing practice of lovingly saying "I do" to *all* of this – come what may, every single day.

COMMITMENT

I choose my life – every day!

Commitment is the unfailing faith in my Higher Power, and unequivocally and wholeheartedly choosing love and life every single day. I've found that commitment is really what seals it all – it is the ultimate gift to myself – a promise to relentlessly practice all the insights gained and shared throughout this book.

Commitment in action is:

– Believing *before* seeing: knowing the possibility of invention, and having faith in faith itself;

– Starting over every single moment, choosing love and choosing life each time, doing the highest and best in this moment, again and again;

– Mustering the courage, when necessary, to tightly but lovingly close doors without vacillation or equivocation, trusting that healthy pruning is necessary for unexpected, expansive openings of opportunity and creative energy;

– Choosing to tell only the present, essential and empowering story about myself, unleashing the creative force that births the immediate future;

– Saying "I do" from within, realizing that commitment is not what I can find outside myself, from another person, but only from within my own center.

Commitment is what continuously deepens my own insights. Every time I stumble off the path, I remember and recommit to my own discoveries and truths. By centering myself I am reminded of my Higher Power right here within me. So, I find consciousness. Compassion, choice, and connectedness open up thereafter, and once again, I have access to my creativity, the ability to create life all over again.

If centering, consciousness, compassion, choice, and connectedness help me receive all the signs from my Higher Power, and creativity enables me to channel it into physical reality, then commitment is what allows me to do this again and again, every single day. I commit, therefore I thrive!

CLOSE

My life is love, my love is god...my god is life

CLOSE

"…When it's over, I want to say all my life
I was a bride married to amazement.
I was the bridegroom, taking the world into my arms."

– Mary Oliver in *"When Death Comes"*

When I started writing *Thrive!* I had absolutely no idea that it would unfold as a love story! It all began with a terrible urgency to write down a key insight I had in June 2009 after attending an advocacy training session for 'survivors' of domestic violence. And this insight was: *the surviving-mindset is antithetic to thriving*, a theme that emerges repeatedly through the stories I share in this book. I realized that so long as the conversation focuses on the dichotomy of survivor-ship and perpetrator-ship, and on the storytelling around survival, we will simply replace old chains and masks with new ones that obscure our true inner light, and prevent us from connecting with the world of possibility. The way to *thrive* is to make a quantum leap, and like the sand mandala art of Buddhist monks, keep wiping the slate clean, and keep writing the new story, the one that creates possibility. So, thriving requires transcending the survival mindset, by consciously and lovingly leaning into (a metaphoric) death! I returned home to somehow capture this idea, and out came pouring the entire outline of *Thrive!* as you see it today!

It wasn't until I was deep into writing, filling out the colors and forms in the scaffold I had outlined, that the true, creative force behind the book – love – came shining through. As I wrote and wrote, I saw the arc of the love story emerge. I had started by awakening to my purer, truer nature, seeing it reflected in my twin soul, Andrew, falling in love at once with both him and myself. This compelled me to break down and break through to my Higher Power. My heart stayed cracked open with love, and I began to see that the love I experienced through the twin soul connection was really a love mediated by the divine, the force of *creation*, something the Sufis told us a long time ago! Now was enabled the blossoming of a full-blown love story, one which connected me in love not only with my own purer nature and creativity, but also with other beings and *their* creativity… with all humanity and human creative potential. So, ultimately, *Thrive!* is about falling in love, with creation, with life. Simply put, life = love = divine = creation = life. To thrive is to create with love and awareness, every moment, every breath, every idea, every endeavor, every manifestation.

Thriving has the energetic quality of *'creating in the flow of,'* while surviving has the energetic quality of '*making it in spite of*.' Thriving seeks to *create life*, which is a love-based endeavor, while surviving seeks to *avert death*, which is a fear-driven endeavor. Thriving is about courage, acting organically and powerfully from the loving heart, while surviving is about bravery, working willfully and forcefully from the calculating mind. So, paradoxically, thriving involves *dying* to many things: past, future, place, time, story, ego, mind, identity, affiliations, position, title, role, external power...and other self-constructs often associated with the surviving mindset.

Weaving together all my insights from the seven chapters, I've come to see the following as essential hallmarks of a thriving life:

Thriving is *always* about acting in love

In a thriving life, all choices are founded in love. "Am I acting in love or in fear?" I ask myself at every turn, and each time I choose love as the motivating and creative force, I thrive. A thriving life is rooted in the love-purpose of the soul. It respects the body temple, and allows the mind to serve the purpose of the soul rather than drive life.

Thriving is a recognition of the divine within

Thriving is about knowing that my Higher Power is always right here within me, in my center of gravity. In a thriving life, I am grateful for my *Wholeness* and *Abundance*, and I'm in *Resonance* with the Universe. This power within my own center has the tremendous ability to self-heal, self-guide and self-transform, and ultimately, to create...everything from nothing. It always knows best, and it always shows me the right way.

Thriving is founded in the 'unreasonable'

A thriving life transcends the rational, logical or obligatory, and locates itself in the realm of the 'unreasonable.' The only impetus at every turn is: "Because I must"! In living, acting and creating in this inspired way, one frequently breaks convention and may be viewed and treated as 'insane,' 'weird,' 'deviant,' and so on; so, all need for approval or validation from others must be completely relinquished.

Thriving is always in the present

Thriving has everything to do with the present; it practically doesn't recognize the past or the future. It knows eternal time, which is accessible through the Now. And like employing the mind in the service of the soul, a thriving life employs linear time solely for the practical purposes of executing creative action and solving problems in the physical dimension.

Thriving is fun and easy!

A thriving life is fun, joyful, delightful and inspiring. And it is *easy*! It is easy not in the least in terms of circumventing hard work, but in the highest and best sense: Time stops still, I forget myself and I get in the zone. The challenges faced in a thriving life result in positive, 'creative exhaustion,' rather than the 'drama exhaustion' that comes from frustrating and depleting uphill climbs, upstream swims, or endless treadmill cycles.

Thriving is a quiet, relentless inner *jihad*

In a thriving life, there is awareness that the true obstacles to be overcome are all within, even when they appear as external circumstances. These obstacles are rooted in fear and its various avatars: ego, resistance, non-forgiveness, false self-constructs, negative beliefs, and so on. A quiet, relentless inner *jihad* ensues – that which the Sufis have called the real or greater *jihad* – a vigilant awareness of negativity, which is constantly and continuously replaced by light and love.

Thriving is creative and generative

Thriving is an uncompromising practice of revealing, exercising and manifesting my highest potential. A thriving life happens *through* me, not *to* me. The divine channels Herself through me (and through you), and so ultimately, I am the creator of my own life. This becomes possible when I take full responsibility (without blame) for everything that happens in my life. I understand my talents and strengths to be mine, yet at the same time, not mine; rather they are instruments for the divine to create through me and become conscious of Herself.

Thriving is about something larger than oneself

A thriving life is always making something larger than itself, converting imaginative ideas into purposeful action for the benefit of others. It is generative; it is connective; it is creative. It creates foundational frameworks for others to build on, to heal with, to be inspired, moved and delighted by, to be transformed through, and so on. The purpose of a thriving life always relates to the higher good, to The One: the connected, collective consciousness that is the aggregate of all souls.

Thriving is about choosing life by *dying before you die*

A thriving life is a commitment to making living a conscious action, starting over every single day. This means that thriving is about *dying before you die*: dying to past and future, dying to self-concept, dying to story, dying to labels and identity…and all other baggage accumulated over linear time that keeps forming false constructs of 'self.' When such a death is died and new possibility invented every single day, one is thriving!

Thriving is about designing death!

Ultimately, then, a thriving life is an active, conscious preparation for a beautiful, honest, and enlightened passing into the next realm. No matter what one believes about what happens after physical death, thriving is about welcoming that transitional moment in the state of the highest consciousness – choosing and creating the experience of passing from one form to another – and the journey of the soul thereafter.

EPILOGUE

EPILOGUE

"The secret of life is to die before you die."

– Eckhart Tolle, *The Power of Now*

Today is the thirty-seventh anniversary of my birth. Picture a newborn – whole, complete and abundant – containing all the necessary intelligence in each and every cell, her full potential contained therein. She is innately wise, fully connected with the divine. She is so attuned through her body-spirit intelligence, that she can tell simply by temperature and vibrations whether her mother is asleep or awake!

Then she begins 'growing up.' She begins to learn 'the word': accumulating language, theoretical knowledge, memories, stories, and all sorts of other baggage. Sometime in her life, though, she might hit such a point of immense suffering that she breaks down enough to drop her baggage and break through. (Or she may receive this breakthrough as an unexpected gift, through no apparent catalyzing event at all.) And if she is fortunate enough to break through, she realizes that she must now *unlearn* everything. She must peel it all away, shed, edit, prune, sculpt…on and on and on…until her own inner light and love, obscured thus far with all the baggage, can shine forth. Now she is 'born again,' accessing the Higher Power that she was gifted at birth, but had forgotten all about. It is now that she has begun *thriving*!

The trick of transcending the mind – transcending survival and making the quantum leap through the wormhole into thriving – is to periodically unlearn everything one has been taught and believes one knows, and then explore freely, like a true traveler, with one's own awakened consciousness. I offer that this is what being 'born again' means. So, while it might seem strange to talk about death on my birthday, I am absolutely delighted and inspired to do so! This is because it is clear as crystal to me as I celebrate life today that truly living – thriving – is really about dying! Dying to the past, dying to self-concept, dying to story, dying to identity…and all other false constructs of 'self' such as "this is me" and "that is not me," which we hold on to out of fear, for the sake of survival. I offer again, that this is the allegorical significance of Jesus's crucifixion and later resurrection. He demonstrated to us through his immense sacrifice that we must die before we die in order to live in our divine potential!

And this brings me to a realization of profound significance: Every word in this book must also die! This is because as soon as my insights, revelations and arising truths are articulated through the limited framework of language, which is nothing but an aggregate of mental constructs, they become learnable, analyzable and convertible into stories, theories and other such identified entities, generating more baggage to feed the mind's addictions, and more hindrances to moment-to-moment thriving! This is why, the literal studying or learning of others' verbal or written frameworks for spiritual experience and insights, including doctrine of all organized religion, can ultimately thwart connecting with one's own Higher Power to lead a thriving life! It is no wonder that the ultimate offering by many highly evolved saints and spiritual leaders is simply a *darshan*: a wordless viewing to bless and hug and impart divine energy!

So, my final insight through practicing the art of thriving is that this soul-experience is yours and yours alone to be had. It can *only* be experienced firsthand, through accessing your own connection with your Higher Power, which is why we all have unique, singular lives. Your thriving life will have your own version of the framework I have described for myself – Centering, Consciousness, Compassion, Choice, Creativity, Connectedness and Commitment – or not. We are each gifted with the same incredible ability, the same direct, unmediated connection with the divine, and we must each follow our own paths to an awakened and thriving life.

Why then, this book? Why bother to write with such intensity and passion for over two years, only to tell you now that every word must die? Because, it is less an offering of words, and more a labor of love, an offering of positive, creative energy. Like a woman pregnant with her creation who *must* give birth, I must deliver this book into the world, as an expression of creativity, connectedness, and commitment, a gift of compassion and love. So, with a humbling awareness of the limitations of the written word for this act of creation and sharing, I offer you this gift. I believe that if you are reading this book, it is because you are either on the brink of coming into your very own thriving life, or are already embodying it; otherwise this book would not have found you! Therefore, you will be able to look beyond the words themselves, and connect and resonate with the intention, love, energy, and power *behind* the words. You will embrace the love and allow the words to die!

This book began with an account of the day on which I had wanted to die, and magically, I succeeded: in dying to the past! That was the day I was reborn. Today, on the otherwise insignificant anniversary of my bodily birth, I renew my commitment to dying to the past, and to being reborn every day. Every sunrise brings a new birthday!

Shahana Dattagupta
May 31, 2011

GRATITUDE

GRATITUDE

"As we express our gratitude, we must never forget that the highest appreciation is not to utter words, but to live by them."

– John F. Kennedy

I'm terribly grateful to many people, named and unnamed, for so many different things that have made living this life and writing this book not only possible, but also necessary, purposeful, loving and joyful.

I'd like to thank all those whose written works on a variety of related and unrelated subjects have inspired, moved, illuminated, and guided me. They are: Melody Beattie (*Beyond Co-Dependency: And Getting Better All the Time*, 1989); Stephan Bodian (*Wake up Now*, 2008), Rhonda Byrne (*The Secret*, 2006); Kevin Carroll (*Rules of the Red Rubber Ball: Find and Sustain Your Life's Work*, 2005); Neil Crofts (*Magic Monday Newsletters*, ongoing); Gurucharan Das (*The Difficulty of Being Good*, 2009); Patti Digh (*Life is a Verb*, 2008); Robert D. Enright (*Forgiveness is a Choice*, 2001); Erich Fromm (*The Art of Loving*, 1956); Seth Godin (*The Dip: A Little Book that Teaches You When to Quit*, 2007; *Tribes*, 2009; *Linchpin: Are You Indispensable?*, 2010; *Seth Godin Blog*, ongoing); Elizabeth Gilbert (*Eat, Pray, Love*, 2006; *Committed*, 2010); Chip and Dan Heath (*Made to Stick: Why Some Ideas Die and Others Survive*, 2007; *Switch: How to Change Things When Change is Hard*, 2010); Hermann Hesse (*Siddhartha*); Howard Mann (*Brickyard Blog*, ongoing); Jiddu Krishnamurti (*Freedom from the Known*; 1975); Hugh Macleod (*Ignore Everybody: and 39 Other Keys to Creativity*, 2009; *Evil Plans*, 2011; *gapingvoid Blog*, ongoing); M. Scott Peck (*The Road Less Traveled*, 2003); Dave Pollard (*Finding the Sweet Spot: The Natural Entrepreneur's Guide to Responsible, Sustainable, Joyful Work*, 2008); Steven Pressfield (*Do the Work*, 2011); Ken Robinson (*The Element: How Finding Your Passion Changes Everything*, 2009); Tim Sanders (*Love is the Killer App: How to Win Business and Influence Friends*, 2002); Bernie S. Siegel (*Prescriptions for Living*, 1998); Richard Skerritt (*Tears and Healing*, 2005); Henry David Thoreau (*Life Without Principle*, 1863); Eckhart Tolle (*The Power of Now*, 1999; *A New Earth*, 2008); Neal Donald Walsch (*Conversations with God: An Uncommon Dialogue*, 1996); Benjamin Zander and Rosamund Stone Zander (*The Art of Possibility*; 2000); and Gary Zukav (*The Seat of the Soul*, 1990).

I'd like to thank the following family, friends, mentors, colleagues and creative partners for their love, inspiration, blessings, guidance, support and collaboration in the last seven years of awakened life-practice: Saara Ahmed, Tiyash Bandyopadhyay, Trisha Barua,

Manoj and Rita Biswas, Joshua Brevoort, Blaine and Heather Brownell, Lisa Chun, Laura Curry, Devasmita Chakraverty, Ashok and Priyam Das, Bonnie Duncan, Tammy Felkner, Scott Francis, Elizabeth Friesen, Bidisha Ghosh, Nilima Ghosh, Rupamanjari Ghosh, Christian and Kristie Grange, Robb Hamilton, Jason Haskins, Cameron Hall, Keith Hui, Srivani Jade, Mickey Kander, Paula Kirkpatrick, Sandeep Krishnamurty, Margaret Lee, Nancy Lim, Amrita Madan, Arijit Mahanalabis, Robert Mankin, Charles Martin, Buffy and Jeff McCune, Rita Meher, Larry Miggins, Bipasha Mukherjee, (Late) Meenakshi Mukherjee, Rohini Mukherjee, Paj Nandi, Sangeeta Naidu, Raman Narayanan, Farah Nousheen, Ana Pinto Da Silva, Arshiya Quadri, Smriti Rai, Meenakshi Rishi, Shaline Samy, Lisa Sebright, Lynne Shira, Checha Sokolovic, Megan Strawn, Samuel Stubblefield, Trisna Tanus, Jay and Schuyler Thoman, Naveen Valluri, Ruchita Varma, Rachael Victoria, Lori Walker, Jonathan Ward, Tully Wehr, Anya Woestwin, all the inspiring women of *Yoni ki Baat* in Seattle, all my *Guru-bandhu* of the Mewati Gharana and Gurukul, and all my creative collaborators at The ACT Theater, Chaya, Pratidhwani, The Seattle Asian Art Museum, The Wing Luke Museum, and Tasveer.

Various people generously facilitated mini 'writing retreats' to support the final hours of labor to birth this book into the world. For this I thank Priyam Das, Bipasha Mukherjee, Naveen Valluri, and Jason Week. Heartfelt thanks to my sister Sharmishtha, Harold Soans and Archana Verma for undertaking invaluable reviews of the first draft, to Nitika Raj for letting me source her collection of quotes, to Farah Abdul, Nimisha Ghosh-Roy, Sheeba Jacob, Sudha Nandagopal, and Archana Verma for their creative input, and to Siddhartha Saha, for his thoughtful and caring photography and videography.

With deep reverence, I thank my Gurus Pandita Tripti Mukherjee ('*Guruji*') and Sangeet Martand Pandit Jasraj ('*Bade Guruji*') for their blessings and faith in me and my creative path.

I thank Robb Hamilton and Rachael Victoria for being my chosen family. I thank Jason Week for the mutual learning through an important time of partnership, and for always supporting my choice. I thank David Gibson for creating a space for healing and higher consciousness. I thank Sabina Ansari and my sister Sharmishtha for being my soulmates and co-travelers in this special journey.

My eternal gratitude extends to my friend and partner Shirin Subhani, not only for her loving editorial work on this book and her unfailing faith and support throughout this and numerous other *Flying Chickadee* projects, but also for being a committed partner in collective creativity and contribution to the world.

I feel incredibly grateful for the unconditional love and support I received from my parents Ranu and Sushanta, and my sister Sharmishtha, in undertaking this soul-baring project. The tremendous courage and openheartedness they have shown in their willingness to be subjects of my writing and explorations is nothing short of a blessing. Through this collective courage, we have transcended the narrative of the past, and have authentically evolved into a loving family.

To give thanks to Andrew McCune seems almost silly, but how can I not? I am so grateful that my twin soul and I traverse the Earth concurrently in time and space! I'm blessed for the divine opportunity to continue evolving to our highest and best by looking in the mirror of each other, listening intently, creating purposefully, and loving unconditionally. I thank Andrew for generously and unquestioningly consenting to the inclusion of my insights from our interactions, throughout this book.

Last but never the least, my cuddly thanks go to two lovely felines, Lailah and Sid, who teach me daily about unconditional love and contentment with the present.